Praise for Alan Ryan's *On Politics*

"Magisterial. . . . In more than a thousand pages, Alan Ryan, a longtime Oxford professor who now teaches at Princeton, undertakes to introduce the reader to most of the major political thinkers in Western history. . . . The tensions of modern liberal democratic societies are the intellectual motor of the book. . . . [L]ively and intellectually engaging. . . . *On Politics*, like the great works of philosophy it examines, constitutes a powerful brief against the unexamined life."

—Adam Kirsch, *The New Yorker*

"Ryan's book is a magnificent piece of work, clear . . . and engaging. . . . [T]he reader is wonderfully caught up in an uninterrupted trajectory of thought. . . . [A]nyone remotely interested in political theory will profit from reading or dipping into Ryan's *On Politics*. . . . The amazing thing about Alan Ryan is that he has assembled so much of this in a single place, so accessible in this two-volume reservoir of historical and political knowledge. . . . It's a remarkable experience."

—Jeremy Waldron, *New York Review of Books*

"Epic. . . . *On Politics* comes crammed with smart observations and wise advice. Readers unfamiliar with figures such as Machiavelli, Montaigne, Montesquieu and Marsilius of Padua, or with scores of lesser-known political writers, will profit from its clear explanations and well-crafted prose."   —John Keane, *Financial Times*

"One of the many merits of Alan Ryan's monumental new history of political philosophy is that it restores our enthusiasm for politics. . . . Mr Ryan's historical approach helps us at the very least to look at our problems from new angles, and at best to harness the help of history's sharpest minds in producing policies. . . . [A]n impressive achievement: an enjoyable mental workout and an admirable monument to a lifetime of academic toil."   —*The Economist*

"Spanning more than 2,500 years, Ryan's masterpiece (he's been working on it for more than three decades) frames the entire history of Western political thinking in the tension between two ideas: personal liberty and responsibility to the state."

—David Ulin, *Los Angeles Times*

"Any intelligent general reader would learn much from this work and from the author's way of thinking about politics. . . . *On Politics* is an outstanding and original work."   —Oliver Kamm, *Times* (London)

"Provocative, illuminating and entertaining—an exemplary work of philosophy and history whose author's deep learning is lightly worn."   —*Kirkus Reviews*

"Remarkably detailed yet highly readable. . . . [C]ontemporary American politics lurk in the background, as Ryan, in this absorbing and edifying read, regularly reminds us of what modern citizens might gain from a deeper understanding of the roots of today's political ideals and loyalties."   —*Publishers Weekly*, starred review

ABOUT THE SERIES:

In *On Politics*, Alan Ryan distilled nearly a half century's career of teaching political theory into a two-volume history of Western political thought that spans three thousand years of history from ancient Greece to the present. Each volume pairs Ryan's trenchant analysis with a biography of a major philosopher, a timeline of their life, as well as key excerpts from their most essential works.

The series includes: *On Aristotle, On Machiavelli, On Tocqueville, On Marx, On Augustine,* and *On Hobbes.*

ALSO BY ALAN RYAN

On Politics: A History of Political Thought: From Herodotus to the Present

Liberal Anxieties and Liberal Education

John Dewey and the High Tide of American Liberalism

Bertrand Russell: A Political Life

Property

Property and Political Theory

J. S. Mill

The Philosophy of the Social Sciences

The Philosophy of John Stuart Mill

ON MACHIAVELLI

The Search for Glory

ALAN RYAN

LIVERIGHT PUBLISHING CORPORATION

A Division of W. W. Norton & Company
New York / London

Portions previously published in *On Politics: A History of Political Thought: From Herodotus to the Present*

Manufacturing by Courier Westford
Book design by Ellen Cipriano
Production manager: Anna Oler

Library of Congress Cataloging-in-Publication Data

Ryan, Alan, 1940–
On Machiavelli : the search for glory / Alan Ryan. — First Edition
pages cm
"Portions previously published in On politics : a history of political thought
from Herodotus to the present"—Title page verso.
Includes bibliographical references and index.
ISBN 978-0-87140-705-4 (hardcover)
1. Machiavelli, Niccolò, 1469–1527. 2. Machiavelli, Niccolò, 1469–1527—
Influence. 3. Political science—Philosophy—History. I. Ryan, Alan,
1940– On politics. II. Title.
JC143.M4R93 2014
320.1092—dc23

2013031499

ISBN 978-1-63149-058-3 pbk.

Liveright Publishing Corporation
500 Fifth Avenue, New York, N.Y. 10110
www.wwnorton.com

W. W. Norton & Company Ltd.
Castle House, 75/76 Wells Street, London W1T 3QT

1 2 3 4 5 6 7 8 9 0

CONTENTS

Preface   7

Chronology   9

Introduction   13

Machiavelli: The Search for Glory   35

Selections   95

    A Note on the Selections   95

    Letter of Niccolò Machiavelli to
    Francesco Vettori, 10 December 1513   97

    The Prince   100

    Discourses   161

PREFACE

In the introduction to *On Politics*, I suggested that one measure of the book's success would be the readers who went and read the works of the authors I discussed. Some readers suggested that I might encourage them to do so by taking chapters of *On Politics* and adding to them substantial extracts from the works I hoped they would read. What follows is exactly that, with a short introduction to provide some of the context that the chapter's original placement in *On Politics* would have provided. As before, I am grateful to Bob Weil and William Menaker at Liveright, as well as to the Norton production team, for their help in making an author's life as easy as it can plausibly be made. I should also acknowledge how indebted I am to Sheldon Wolin, Isaiah Berlin, Quentin Skinner, and Maurizio Viroli for their penetrating insights into Machiavelli.

CHRONOLOGY

59 BCE	Florence founded by Julius Caesar
421 CE	Legendary date of the foundation of Venice
697	Election of first doge of Venice
1070–1115	Tuscany ruled by Countess Matilda
1115	Florence emerges as a commune on Matilda's death
1115	Siena ruled by its bishop
1167	Siena frees itself from episcopal control
1125–82	Florence expands and conquers surrounding countryside
1172	Establishment of Grand Council by Venice
1204	Sack of Constantinople by Fourth Crusade on behalf of Venice
1216	Feud between Guelphs and Ghibellines begins in Florence
1260	Siena defeats Florence at Battle of Montaperti
1293	The Ordinances of Justice passed by Florence

1297	The *serrata* (closing) of the Venetian Grand Council
1300	Florentine Guelphs split into Black and White factions; Dante, a White, is exiled
1348	Black Death
1378	Revolt of the *ciompi* (textile workers); political concessions made and withdrawn
1434	Cosimo de' Medici becomes de jure ruler of Florence until his death in 1464
1469	Machiavelli born, May 3
1471	Election of Pope Sixtus IV
1484	Election of Pope Innocent VIII
1492	Election of Pope Alexander VI; death of Lorenzo de' Medici and accession of Piero de' Medici
1494	French invasion of Italy; French troops enter Florence; Piero de' Medici and the Medici family expelled; Girolamo Savonarola urges restoration of the republic
1497	The Bonfire of the Vanities, February 7; Savonarola excommunicated by Pope Alexander VI, May 12; Florence threatened with papal interdict if the city continues to harbor Savonarola
1498	Savonarola tried for heresy; hanged and burned at the stake, May 23; Florentine Republic reestablished; Machiavelli appointed second chancellor by the Grand Council in June and secretary of the Ten of War in July

1501–10	Florence wages war to recapture Arezzo and Pisa
1502	Piero Soderini elected *gonfaloniere* for life
1512	Florentine Republic suppressed by papal and Spanish forces; Machiavelli dismissed and confined to Florentine territory
1513	February, Machiavelli arrested and tortured; on release in March, Machiavelli retires to his farm at Percussina; Giovanni de' Medici elected as Pope Leo X; July, Machiavelli begins to write *The Prince* and to draft *Discourses on Livy*, which he reads to friends
1518	Writes *The Art of War*, published 1521; writes his satirical play *Mandragola*
1518–19	*Discourses on Livy* completed
1520	Cardinal Giulio de' Medici (later Clement VII) commissions his *Florentine Histories*
1525	*Mandragola* performed in Venice; Machiavelli visits Rome to present his *Florentine Histories* to Pope Clement VII
1527	Sack of Rome by imperial forces; the Florentine Republic restored in May; Machiavelli dies June 21, and is buried in Santa Croce
1530	The Medici again restored to power; Alessandro de' Medici becomes duke of Tuscany
1531–32	Publication of *The Prince*, *Discourses on Livy*, and *Florentine Histories*
1555	Florence annexes Siena
1797	Fall of the republic of Venice

INTRODUCTION

THE DECADE DURING WHICH Machiavelli wrote, but could not publish, his two great contributions to political thinking was an extraordinary one both in the history of political thinking and in European political and military history. Our concern is with the former, but Machiavelli's own concerns were with the latter until he was forced to be a spectator of events he could not influence. In 1513 Machiavelli began work on *The Prince*, in 1516 Thomas More published *Utopia*, and in 1517 Martin Luther nailed his ninety-five theses to the door of the cathedral of Wittenberg. Machiavelli's beloved Florentine Republic, which he had served since 1498, was overthrown by the combined forces of Spain and the papacy in 1512, and the exiled Medici were restored to power. He set about writing *The Prince* sometime after April 1513, after being released from the Bargello prison, where the new regime had had him interrogated under torture; he was wrongly but not implausibly suspected of involvement in a plot to restore Piero Soderini to power and send the Medici into exile once again. As his letter to Francesco Vettori suggests, he had made a lot of progress by the end of 1513, but he must have thought the work finished only after March 1516 when Giuliano de' Medici died, and Machiavelli dedicated the work instead to Lorenzo de' Medici, duke of Urbino. Manuscript copies appear to have circulated around this time.

Thomas More's *Utopia* was a work at the opposite end of the spectrum from Machiavelli's *Prince* and *Discourses*, modeled perhaps on Plato's *Republic*, but with debts to classical comic writers such as Lucian, and surely meant to show his friend Desiderius Erasmus that More was capable of writing the semiserious, self-mocking reflections on the human condition that Erasmus had made in *The Praise of Folly* a few years earlier. Whereas Machiavelli took the desire for power and a hunger for glory as inextinguishable elements in human nature, and the Roman domination of the then known world as the summit of political success, More depicted his Utopians as despising glory, waging war in self-defense, or very occasionally to rescue neighboring peoples from a tyrannical ruler, never to expand their dominion over their neighbors for the mere sake of doing so. Virtuous self-sufficiency was the object, not glory.

More was a devout Roman Catholic, and in 1535 he lost his head to Henry VIII's executioner for his refusal to acknowledge Henry rather than the pope as the head of the English church. The most significant event of the decade of 1510 to 1520 was Martin Luther's lighting the tinder that turned into the all-consuming Reformation; Machiavelli wrote *The Prince* and his *Discourses* too soon to notice; the latter were probably finished in 1518–19, after being read in installments to his friends in the gardens of the Rucellai family. The popes of Machiavelli's adult years—Sixtus VI (1471–84), Innocent VIII (1484–92), Alexander VI (1492–1503), Pius III (September–October 1503), Julius II (1503–13), Leo X (1513–21), Adrian VI (1521–22), and Clement VII (1523–34)—presided over a golden age of Roman music, art, and architecture, but also over the decline of the church's religious authority. In the political realm, they had mixed fortunes; Alexander VI and Julius II were renowned as warrior popes and highly praised for their abilities and all-around ruthlessness by Machiavelli himself, but the papacy's ability to act as an independent military force declined in comparison with that of the major European monarchies. The Sack of Rome by the forces of Charles V in 1527 is conventionally viewed as the end of the papacy's ability to wield effective military power in the Italian peninsula as an independent power, although war between the French and Spanish monarchies continued until 1559, and the Papal States themselves endured as a political entity until 1871, and the final unification of Italy. The success of the papacy in not only keeping but enlarging its territorial possessions in the sixteenth and seventeenth centuries was more a matter of diplomacy than of brute force.

The erosion of the papacy's unique moral and theological authority within Western Christendom was less dramatic than the Sack of Rome, although the human casualties of the more than a century-long sequence of European wars of religion had become enormous by the time the Treaty of Westphalia put an end to the Thirty Years' War in 1648. The Protestant Reformation took hold of different parts of Europe only fitfully, and at the time of Luther's death, in 1546, it was unclear whether a determined assault by Catholic rulers led by the most powerful of them, the emperor Charles V, might not restore religious unity at the point of the sword. The Wars of Religion in France ended with the restoration of a Catholic monopoly and the barest toleration for Protestants; Spain was unshakably and intolerantly Catholic; the Reformation made no headway in Italy. With hindsight, it is unimaginable that there would not have been a new Reformation if Catholicism had triumphed in the sixteenth century; Luther had had many predecessors, most silenced by the executioner and replaced by reformers undeterred by their fate. What provoked Luther to nail his ninety-five theses to the door of Wittenberg cathedral was a direct result of the papacy's role as a secular power, and papal ambitions to regain control of the Papal States and dominate central and northern Italy. To enhance papal revenues, needed both for military purposes and for the rebuilding of St. Peter's, the papacy greatly increased the sale of "indulgences." These amounted to a promise on papal authority that in return for a gift to the church, the purchaser or some beneficiary nominated by the purchaser would have a reduction in the time he must serve in purgatory. This is not the place to delve into the theological issues behind Luther's outrage, or into the further conclusions he drew about the inefficacy of most of the sacraments. It is the place to observe two things relevant to our purposes.

The first is that Machivalli has unkind things to say about the papacy. Although Clement VII licensed the publication of both *The Prince* and the *Discourses* after Machiavelli's death, they were put on the Index of prohibited books as soon as it was established during the Counter-Reformation of the 1550s. Machiavelli's denunciation of the papacy rather than his relish for the cunning of its agent Cesare Borgia was the obvious source of the offense he gave. The papacy, he said, is the great obstacle to the project of reunifying Italy as a military and political force to be reckoned with by the Spanish and French monarchies. It is too powerful to be ignored, too weak to overwhelm its rivals, especially when those rivals would make and break alliances with foreign powers such as France and Spain as well as with the papacy itself. This objection to the papacy is narrowly political, in the sense that it is a complaint against the papacy's position in late fifteenth- and early sixteenth-century Italy rather than its neglect of its religious duties. Machiavelli accuses the papacy of corruption on numerous occasions as well, but almost in passing, knowing as well as anyone that the papal tiara often changed hands for money, that popes secured cardinals' hats for their illegitimate children, and that gifts were lavished on the mistresses of a supposedly celibate clergy.

The second thing to observe is that Machiavelli is in general skeptical about the value of Christianity as a religion that provides a basis for the sort of state he hankers after. It is impossible on the evidence available to know quite what Machiavelli thought about the truth or falsehood of the Christian religion; he never questions its truth, for all his subsequent reputation as an atheist. What he appears to have thought, and in this he was followed by Rousseau, was that the otherworldliness of Christianity was intrinsically a poor basis for the kind of patriotism that the Roman Republic had been able to draw on. To the extent that a devout belief in Christianity was consistent with a devotion to one's *patria* even to the point of a readiness to die in battle for its survival and expansion, it would be the Christianity of the early, pure churches. Oddly enough, this places Machiavelli in the same camp as Luther and subsequent reformers in the English church, whose ecclesiology was based on the desire to recapture the simplicity and piety of the early church, although their motives were religious rather than political.

The context in which Machiavelli lived, worked, and wrote could hardly have been less propitious for his ambitions. At no point since the declining years of the Roman Empire had Italian politics been other than tumultuous, but it was Machivaelli's misfortune to serve a republic whose historical moment was over. In the centuries before Machiavelli's birth in 1460, the peninsula had been subjected to a tug-of-war among multiple forces. The Holy Roman Empire claimed a broad sovereignty over much of northern and central Italy, for the most part ineffectually, but it provided the pretext for many invasions; the papacy unsurprisingly resisted these claims, but had its own problems with the urge for independence felt by many of the towns of the Romagna and Umbria, the northeastern area of Italy that made up a substantial part of the Papal States. French interest in Italy went back to the Angevin kingdom of Naples, initially the Kingdom of the Two Sicilies, embracing both the island and a substantial part of southern Italy, based on Naples. After the successful revolt of the Sicilians in 1282, the so-called Sicilian Vespers, the mainland kingdom was contested between the kings of France and Aragon. Crucially both for the history of Italy and for Machiavelli's career, the kingdom had fallen to the Aragonese in 1458, but on the death of its ruler, Ferrante, in 1494, the French king Charles VIII decided to press his claim to the kingdom by invading Italy. It was the French demand for free passage down the west coast of Italy through Florentine territory, for the surrender of several cities along their route, and for a contribution to their expenses in addition that led to the downfall of Piero de' Medici and the installation of Girolamo Savonarola as ruler of Florence. The next sixty-five years are conventionally described as the period of the Italian wars, although the warfare was European in scope, involving among other things the final eviction of the English from France and Charles V's attempts to bring the territory of the Holy Roman Empire back within the Catholic fold.

Machiavelli had been dead for thirty years by the time the wars ended, and his direct experience of Florentine military and diplomatic affairs ended with the downfall of the republic in 1512. He was a historically minded writer, looking back at the glories of the Roman Republic and contrasting the successes of Rome with the failures of his contemporaries as well as occupied for some of his time in retirement in writing his history of Florence and of Italy on a commission from Cardinal Giulio de' Medici, who later became Pope Clement VII. To set him a little more firmly in his context, a thumbnail sketch of the history of three republics and the Papal States may be useful—Florence because it was the city that he loved more than his own soul; Siena because it was the neighbor, rival, and military foe of Florence; Venice because it provided Machiavelli with the image of a republic built for longevity at the price of curbing the political participation of the great majority of its citizens; and the Papal States because they surrounded Florence on three sides, and in spite of Florence's historical alliance with the papacy against the empire, a wholly independent Florence suited the papacy less than one firmly under papal control. It was Pope Julius II who, allied with the Spanish, reinserted the Medici in Florence in 1512; the reinstalled Giovanni de' Medici became Pope Leo X shortly thereafter, to be succeeded as the ruler of Florence by his brother Giuliano. Giovanni had been made cardinal at the age of thirteen as a favor to his father, Piero, "the Unfortunate." His nephew Lorenzo is the dedicatee of *The Prince*.

It is debatable whether Machiavelli's *History of Flor-*

ence and of the Affairs of Italy is harder to follow as an account of Italian political and military affairs in general, or as an account of the military, political, and constitutional affairs of Florence in particular. Written in the early 1520s, it is full of Machiavelli's characteristic verve, and permeated throughout by his mordant reflections on the "imbecility" of sixteenth-century Italy, but it does not display the fastidious concern for chronological transparency that a modern historian would try to achieve. It is hard to complain. The history of the Florentine Republic from the twelfth century to the sixteenth was entangled in the history of Italy at large, and that was a history of shifting alliances, agreements made and broken, successful political ventures cut short by sudden death, and periods of prosperity interrupted by warfare, famine, drought, and plague, the worst of which was the Black Death in 1348, after which the population of Florence and many other cities never regained its former level.

To the extent that it was able, Florence governed itself as a sovereign republic; this is not to say that it was what a modern eye would recognize as a democracy, although it was a more participatory political system than most. The city's foundation in 59 BCE by Julius Caesar was a source of civic pride, but irrelevant to its medieval and subsequent history. The Florence that Machiavelli knew began with humble origins as a colony established by the neighboring city of Fiesole, to serve according to Machiavelli's own conjecture as a marketplace on level ground below the hilltop town. The Florentine Republic dominated the area of modern Tuscany, the territory that became the duchy and then the grand duchy of Tuscany after the final extirpation of the republic in 1537. From what is usually recognized as the foundation of the city as a commune in 1115, Florence expanded during the twelfth century, in spite of periodic attempts by successive occupants of the throne of the Holy Roman Empire to reassert imperial authority over their Italian domains. The city built on the prosperity derived from its textile industry and its early start in providing banking services for much of Europe to expand across Tuscany, establishing direct rule over smaller cities in the region or neutralizing their ability to expand on their own account. Florence's rule was never entirely stable or unchallenged. Its need for access to the Mediterranean meant that cities such as Lucca and Pisa were a standing problem, and a great deal of Machiavelli's time as secretary of the Ten of War was occupied in prosecuting the nearly interminable war with Pisa.

The city's internal politics were as difficult as its external relations. As with all Italian city republics, one persistent difficulty was the rivalry of great families, each of which believed it had a claim to monopolize power; this might in itself have led in time to a stable aristocratic government with several families sharing government positions, although the history of many Italian states equally suggests that it would have been wishful thinking to expect such an outcome. In any case, the raw materials for such a system of turn and turn about were lacking. Florence was a commercial and financial state, property was less easily preserved and passed down through the generations than the landed property of northern feudal aristocrats, and hereditary authority was late in arriving. For much of the thirteenth century, the Gueph and Ghibelline factions, broadly populist and aristocratic rather than strictly pro-church and pro-empire, alternated in power, allying themselves with other cities, exiling their opponents, and rarely enjoying long periods of unchallenged authority. In 1293 Florence passed the Ordinances of Justice, which set up a republican constitution based on the guilds that organized the city's economic life. Between 1328 and 1434, and again during the short-lived republic of 1498–1512, Florence adopted a relatively open system of government, using sortition to ensure something close to a random selection of city officers from among the better-off families of the city, drawn from the six districts into which the city was divided. For short periods, eligibility was widened further to include small merchants and artisans. Even after

1434, when Cosimo de' Medici established himself as the unchallenged ruler of Florence, he took care to rule within the forms of a republican constitution, although he took equal care to ensure that enough of those citizens whose support mattered were literally or figuratively in his debt.

The longest period of stability was provided by the rule of the Medici family. The Medici were bankers, and their prosperity owed a good deal to the misfortunes of rival banking families both in Siena and in Florence. Cosimo de' Medici was something of a political genius; he rescued Florence from a potentially disastrous war with Naples by going in person to Naples to negotiate peace, and he preserved his power by exercising it unobtrusively. Like other city-states, Florence was governed by a system of committees, answerable to officers chosen by lot from the citizens at large. The goal, of course, was to keep anyone from exercising too much influence; if we choose our rulers by lottery, their election cannot be rigged. The trick for anyone who wished to ensure that their men governed was to make certain that only the right names went into the bag from which the members of the ruling elite were drawn. It was the rule of the Medici family that came to an end in 1494 when Piero the Unfortunate made his disastrous treaty with the French, returned to Florence to meet the *signoria* and was driven out of the city. There then followed the attempt to institute a republic of virtue, led by Girolamo Savonarola, which fell afoul of the papacy's hostility to Savonarola's reforming zeal, expressed in blazing sermons and in spectacles such as the famous Bonfire of the Vanities in February 1497, when rich Florentines threw valuables ranging from books and works of art to their best clothes into the flames. In 1498 Savanarola was deposed, tried for heresy, strangled, and burned at the stake. For the next fourteen years Florence was a republic, loyally served by Machiavelli.

Venice and Siena form counterparts to Florence in different ways. Siena was a neighbor and a rival of Florence; it might, but for the accidents of the banking business, have become another Florence. Paradoxically, Siena endured as an independent republic more than two decades longer than Florence, only to fall in 1555 to the combined forces of Spain and Florence, and to be incorporated within the duchy of Florence in settlement of the debts of the Spanish crown to the Medici. Like Florence, Siena was part of the imperial Italian domain before seizing its independence in 1115; initially, Siena was governed by a prince-bishop, but by 1179 the bishop's authority had been repudiated and a secular republican constitution established, and much as in Florence, power was slowly acquired by the ordinary citizens and lost by its former aristocratic possessors. Much as in Florence, the city gained control of the surrounding countryside; again, much as in Florence, the city was internally divided both between the better-off and the worse-off and between the inhabitants of the different districts of the city. Since Florence was always the main external enemy, in the conflicts of Guelph and Ghibelline, Ghibelline Siena commonly faced Guelph Florence. Siena was initially even more important than Florence to the development of a European banking system, and if the Bonsignori bank had not failed at the end of the thirteenth century as a result of the conflict between the papacy and the French monarchy, Siena might have held its position indefinitely. In military terms, the Sienese had proved more than a match for Florence: the Battle of Montaperti in 1260 had seen a much smaller army of Sienese reinforced by the German cavalry of King Manfred utterly rout the Florentine forces. The collapse of the Gran Tavola, or Bonsignori bank, was followed by other banking collapses, and like many cities Siena never fully recovered from the Black Death in 1348. Had Florence not been weakened, and had Siena not had allies that made it more formidable, the end might well have come long before 1555.

Although Venice was very much larger than Siena or Florence, and endured as a republic until 1797, when Napoleon peremptorily swept it away along with many other elderly but no longer formidable institutions, the importance of Venice for our purposes is limited to one aspect of its politics. Venice had begun, as Machiavelli reminds his readers in many places, as a collection of fishing villages seeking the protection of their watery environment against Lombard invaders. Initially owing a somewhat notional allegiance to the Byzantine Empire, Venice developed its own institutions from the eighth century onwards. Machiavelli treats Venice as the paradigm of a political system designed for longevity, as did subsequent writers influenced by Machiavelli such as the seventeenth-century English republican theorist Sir James Harrington. The contrast that underlay their interest was between a state whose aim was longevity and one whose aim was expansion; in the light of Venice's development into a maritime power that dominated the eastern Mediterranean for several centuries, it seems surprising to classify Venice as a state built for endurance rather than for empire, but two aspects of Venetian constitutional arrangements explain what is at stake.

The Venetians went to all lengths to ensure that the head of state, the doge, could not be installed by a faction or govern in the interests of a factional group of one sort or another. The elaborate system of election, involving successive rounds of choice by lot and election, is mind-boggling in its complexity. What impressed observers more, however, was the decision made in 1297 to permanently confine eligibility for

membership of the Grand Council, from which officeholders and governing committees were chosen, to the
families entitled to membership at that date. The *serrata*,
or locking, of the constitution endured for the next six
and a quarter centuries. It ensured that Venice did not
succumb to the factional infighting that plagued Florence and Siena, although skeptics might think that
other features of Venetian life such as the efficiency of
the secret police played a significant role in preventing
internal dissension. It was also true that Venetian government was efficient. The Grand Council had a very
large membership, and effective executive authority
rested with the senate of between forty and sixty members, as well as with numerous committees; the model
thus established a head of state, a senate, and a wider
controlling body that elected officials and provided an
example on which future republican governments were
modeled in the United States, France, and elsewhere.
Nonetheless, one later observer, John Stuart Mill,
thought that Venice was efficient because it had the virtues of a bureaucratic regime as much as those of an
aristocratic one; as a mercantile state, it understood the
nature of sound management. None of this could save
Venice from external problems; after the fall of Con-
stantinople, the Venetian strongholds in Greece, Crete,
and Cyprus were gradually conquered by the Ottoman
Turks, while the rise of the transoceanic empires of

Spain, France, and Britain destroyed Venice's advantage as the western end of the overland route to Asia. In Machiavelli's day, Venice was still a formidable power in northeastern Italy, a useful ally and dangerous enemy, but manifestly past its days of glory.

The greatest danger to Florence during Machiavelli's time as a servant of the Florentine Republic came from the Papal States. The Papal States were not abolished until the reunification of Italy in 1871, but the grip of successive popes on their patrimony was never entirely secure until the end of the Italian wars. The pope was more nearly a feudal suzerain than a political sovereign in the same sense as the kings of France and England. The various cities of the swath of territory extending from Ravenna in the northeast to Rome in the southwest were for much of the time under the control of the local nobility, and their allegiance to their papal superior was nominal at best. Relations between the papacy and the Holy Roman Empire were rarely cordial; the papal domains had initially been a gift from the Frankish king Pepin in 751, confirmed by Charlemagne, and again long afterward by the emperor Otto. But whether this meant that the pope ruled as an agent of the emperor, or that the emperor ruled as an agent of the pope, was endlessly disputed. It was Frankish military force that first secured the papacy's possessions, but the Holy Roman Empire was an invention of the papacy, so the question of political superiority was wide open. During the fourteenth-century removal of the papacy to Avignon, papal authority had been nominal, and Rome itself a battleground for rival aristocratic families, until Cardinal Albornoz succeeded both in imposing papal authority over the Papal States by brute force and in imposing a uniform legal code that survived for four and a half centuries. The crucial issue in Machiavelli's day was once again whether the pope could control the various cities of the Papal States by installing "vicars" or agents under papal authority in place of whatever local ruling families had usurped that authority. Alexander VI and Julius II were remarkably successful in bringing this about in the late fifteenth and early sixteenth centuries; it was Cesare Borgia, the son of Alexander VI, who so impressed Machiavelli with the mixture of cunning and violence that he brought to the task of reconquering the Romagna and pacifying it. From the point of view of a loyal Florentine, of course, the success of Cesare Borgia was almost too impressive, since it was only the self-restraint of the pope that kept papal armies out of Tuscany. The fate of Savonarola testified to the power that the papacy could wield in Florence.

Machiavelli's *Prince* ends with an exhortation to its dedicatee, or anyone with the power to do it, to unite Italy and drive out the barbarians from the country.

Nineteenth-century commentators saw this as an early expression of Italian nationalism, but it was more plausibly an expression of the same hankering after the great days of the Roman Republic than anything so anachronistic as an early expression of nineteenth-century nationalism. Indeed, one oddity of Machiavelli's work is his unconcern with what we today most frequently think of when we think of Rome, Florence, Siena, and Venice. To us, Renaissance Italy is remarkable for its art and architecture, its music and its literature. How this miracle was achieved in the face of near-constant warfare and the constant threat of civil war it is impossible to say; and happily, this is not the place to wonder whether Michelangelo's Sistine Chapel ceiling is a fair return for the wars of religion that were provoked by papal extravagance and the corruption of the Roman curia. The one thing we must observe here is that Machiavelli ignores the artistic and intellectual achievements of the Renaissance almost completely, mentioning the passion for excavating ancient sculpture and making modern versions of the great works of the past only to complain that this contrasts with the unwillingness of the great men of his day to uncover and emulate the deeds of Moses, Theseus, Cyrus, and the other founders of states.

ON MACHIAVELLI

Machiavelli: The Search for Glory

MACHIAVELLI WAS BORN IN 1469 and died in 1527. Little is known about Machiavelli's life before 1498, when he became second chancellor of the Florentine Republic that had been established after the overthrow of Savonarola. This was a "civil service" post. As in classical Athens, political office in the Florentine Republic was held on a brief tenure, and officeholders were either elected or chosen by lot. Without a permanent skilled bureaucracy, Florence would have been ungovernable; Machiavelli was part of that bureaucracy. A month later he was appointed secretary to the Ten of War, the committee that supervised foreign relations and military preparedness. He spent much of the next fourteen years on diplomatic missions to the papal court, to the court of Louis XII in France, and to the court of Emperor Maximilian. Because Florence was friendly to France, it took delicate maneuvering to retain the friendship of the French without incurring the hostility of the empire—to hunt with the Valois without being hounded by the Habsburgs.

In the course of these missions, Machiavelli spent a lot of time with Cesare Borgia in the Romagna and with Pope Julius II, the most warlike of Renaissance popes, whose financial exactions were one of the provocations of Luther's campaign of church reform. The stories that give piquancy to Machiavelli's advice in *The Prince* and the *Discourses on Livy* are often prefigured in his lively correspondence with his masters in Florence. One of Machiavelli's less remembered but important achievements as secretary of the Ten of War was the institution of a Florentine militia recruited from the *contado*, the countryside around Florence. He was hostile to mercenary troops, who, as he pointed out, would desert to the enemy for higher pay if the enemy could offer it, or else subvert the government of their employers. It was an innovation to treat the *contadini* as fit material for warfare; the right to bear arms had been confined to the *cittadini*, the citizen body of Florence itself. Florence's forces were no more of a match for the armies of France or the empire than those of any other Italian state of the day, but Machiavelli's reforms provided an effective militia for local hostilities. The army he created brought the interminable war with Pisa to a successful conclusion.

Machiavelli was not a great figure in the Florentine Republic, but he was well-known, and he took pleasure in doing an impossible job well. He also took pleasure in the fact that his intellect, wit, and erudition made him welcome in upper-class circles from which his origins would otherwise have excluded him. His career, but not these friendships, came to an end in 1512 when Florence's delicate balancing act between papacy, France, and empire proved impossible to sustain, and the republic surrendered to the forces of Ferdinand, the king of Spain, dedicatee of Erasmus's *Panegyric* and predecessor of the emperor Charles V. The Medici were installed as de facto hereditary dukes—though the title was not conferred for another twenty years, and republican forms were initially preserved. Machiavelli was immediately dismissed; it is not clear why, since many colleagues kept their posts, but he was closely associated with Piero Soderini, the foremost spirit of the republic, and Machiavelli's leading role in missions that would ordinarily have been entrusted to aristocrats rather than to bureaucrats reflected Soderini's confidence in him. A little later an abortive plot to assassinate the new rulers was uncovered, and Machiavelli's name was found on a scrap of paper belonging to a conspirator. Arrested on suspicion, he was tortured and jailed, but his innocence was obvious, and he was released a few weeks later.

For the rest of his life, he lived on his farm at Percussina, seven miles from the city, writing and dreaming of a return to public life. Although he was married and had six children, he pined for the excitement of politics. Attempts to find employment with the Medici in Florence or Rome came to nothing, but he secured some writing commissions, and by the time he died was sufficiently in everyone's good graces to be buried in Santa Croce. Nonetheless, only his treatise on the creation and training of a militia, the *Arte della guerra*, was published in his lifetime. *The Prince* was written at breakneck speed in the last six months of 1513, after his release from prison, but published only in 1532. It was the first work to be put on the *Index auctorum et librorum prohibitorum* when that instrument of compulsory intellectual hygiene for adherents of the Catholic faith was created in 1559 by the pope and made permanent in 1564 by the Council of Trent; it was not removed from the Index until the twentieth century and was for many years thought to be so subversive that anyone wishing to read it for purposes of refutation had to ask permission of the pope. Permission was usually refused.

In this enforced retirement, Machiavelli remained a member of the group that met in the gardens of the Rucellai family palazzo in Florence. The *Discourses* was probably written at the request of Cosimo Rucellai, to whom it is dedicated. Like Cicero, Machiavelli thought writing a poor second best to playing an active part in politics; his famous account of the way he would settle down to write by dressing in his state robes and retiring to his study to commune with the immortal dead has a melancholy air. "For four hours I experience no boredom, I forget all my troubles and my fear of poverty, and death holds no more terrors for me."[1] It makes a great difference to what he wrote and how we should read it that Machiavelli was writing practically oriented books. They had to appeal to their dedicatee—*The Prince* was a failed job application—but they bore on one crucial question: how Florence and similar city-states could be governed. Machiavelli's answer was that everything depended on the circumstances. If it were possible to reinstate the Roman Republic, it should be done; if, as seems probable, it is not, we can only hope that a true master of the skills that enable a man to gain power and keep it will arise and establish order. This is not very distant from Bartolus's argument that tyranny may be a necessity in extreme conditions.

THE UNPLACEABILITY OF MACHIAVELLI

Machiavelli has always been an elusive thinker because he was much more (and less) than a "political theorist." This is not because he longed to be active in politics; Cicero is far from unplaceable. It is because he had an astonishing impact on how Europe talked and wrote about politics after his death. Whether he made any impact on the way European politicians acted, as distinct from providing them with a target to criticize for their own hypocritical ends, is unanswerable. Frederick the Great, tongue in cheek, suggested that any ruler who was about to launch an unprovoked attack on his neighbors should first attack Machiavelli. Machiavelli's impact on political rhetoric is undeniable. "Hobbesian" is a term of art familiar to political theorists and political scientists; "Machiavellian" needs no explanation. Whereas "Hobbesian" or "Platonic" carry few pejorative overtones, "Machiavellian" is not a neutral term. The "murderous Machiavel" was a stock figure in Elizabethan drama; and high-minded denunciations of Machiavellianism are to this day part of the standard repertoire of duplicitous politicians who have never read a sentence of his work. On one occasion, President Eisenhower denounced what he took to be Machiavelli's doctrine that "the end justifies the means" without explaining just what might justify the means other than the end.

The popular image of Machiavelli as the "teacher of evil," who praised deceit and violence for their own sake is not the whole truth; most commentators think it is no part of the truth, and few scholars think it is much of the truth. Machiavelli outraged opinion because he took pains to insist that political success demands morally obnoxious acts from anyone seriously engaged in politics. This was not news; it was the lesson the Athenians taught the inhabitants of Melos. It was, however, denied by Stoicism, which was committed to the doctrine that there could be no ultimate conflict between justice and expediency, between the *honestum* and the *utile*.[2] Common sense and everyday political practice in Renaissance Italy suggested that whatever might be true once we take our fate in the hereafter into account, virtue and effectiveness were all too visibly at odds here and now. Our rulers are moved by "reason of state," which is to say the need minimally to "keep the show on the road," and where possible to maximize the state's capacity to enforce order internally and to compete effectively on the international stage. Nonetheless, the readiness to say that political success demanded an unflinching willingness to violate every moral precept appropriate to private life as sharply as Machiavelli did was novel in Christian Europe. Even more unnerving was his seeming uninterest in seeking a justification beyond political success; combating the thought that Romulus's murder of his twin, Remus, was an evil act, he admits that homicide is ordinarily a bad thing and goes on to say that once a city is founded, the freedom to commit such homicides should be denied our rulers. As to Romulus, the result justified the action. Still, "if the means accuse, the end must excuse" is not exactly a moral justification.[3]

Machiavelli's insistence on the tension between the demands of morality and the demands of political practice is more than plausible, but it is unnerving because he left that tension so visibly unresolved. What he intended his readers to feel about it is obscure. It is possible that Machiavelli suffered no more anguish about the tension between the demands of morality and the demands of *raison d'état* than did the Athenians threatening the Melians with massacre, and that he was concerned only to remind his readers of what they knew in their hearts: turning the other cheek may gain the kingdom of heaven but is likely to lose an earthly kingdom. He certainly thought that his fellow Florentines were much too willing to think they were under the peculiar protection of God, and were therefore lackadaisical about their political and military affairs. A sharp reminder of the conflict between Christian virtue and political common sense was what they needed, if not what they wanted.

More than most thinkers, Machiavelli suffers if taken too much out of context. The works we read today—*The Prince* and *Discourses on Livy*—were written to help their author realize his ambition to play a role in Florentine politics, preferably under a republic, but failing that, in any regime that would employ him. Unattractive though the advice offered in *The Prince* may be, Machiavelli's advice to a "new prince" who must stamp his authority on a republic that had prized its liberty had an obvious relevance to the restored Medici family, reinserted by a foreign army in the city that had expelled them eighteen years before.[4] The *Discourses* was written when the Medici were again unpopular, and although Machiavelli died before the short-lived restoration of the republic in 1527–30, a treatise on how the Roman Republic had gained and kept its liberty had obvious resonance. The question whether a state that has once been corrupted can regain its liberty, which preoccupies both works, has an obvious relevance both to the republics of 1494 and 1498 and to the republic of 1527–30. Most of Machiavelli's other works were written to order; *Mandragola*, his louche little play on the theme of foolish husbands, ingenious adulterers, and corrupt friars, was commissioned by Francesco Guicciardini when he was governing Modena on behalf of Leo X; Guicciardini had been Machiavelli's superior in Florence, and managed the transition to a new employer more successfully than he, though not without some personal risk. The *History of Florence* was commissioned by Leo X, the first Medici pope. Leo died before it was finished, and it was presented five years later to Clement VII, the second Medici pope, though published only in 1531. To see how Machiavelli may have expected his work to be read, we need some sense both of the constitutional arrangements and the practical politics of Florence, Florentine relations with the papacy and with the Habsburg and Valois dynasties, the empire and France.

FLORENCE

Florence was constitutionally a popular republic; but for most of the previous century it had been ruled de facto by the Medici family. This situation was not uncommon, but the contrast of republican institutions and more or less covert princely rule was particularly striking in Renaissance Florence. Florence was also a regional power, and its emphasis on *libertas* for citizens of Florence was not reflected in the treatment of the subordinate cities that it controlled. Florentine ideology was at odds with Florentine practice. The ideology held that *liberty* was so vital to the citizens of Florence that they would sooner die than be ruled by a tyrant; practice suggested that as long as the Medici did not *claim* to rule by hereditary right and were good managers, they would be accepted as the rulers of Florence. This is not very different from modern liberal democracies, where professional politicians beget professional politicians, or acquire them as sons- and daughters-in-law, much as law and medicine run in families. Many medieval theorists would have seen the tension between populist theory and monarchical practice as a small matter. As we have seen, the conventional wisdom was that the *regimen regale* was the best of all regimes so long as the "king"—who might be a duke or a count—governed justly, and in the common interest, not his own self-interest. The danger of a *regimen regale* was that it could degenerate into simple tyranny; but constitutional government by one temperate, wise, brave, and just man was best if it could be had. Devout republicans feared that one-man—or one-family—rule would inevitably become simple tyranny; less devout republicans thought that so long as they did not empty the state treasury or murder their rivals without recourse to law it was not truly tyranny. *Some*, but only a minority, of the citizens of Florence thought after the event that Lorenzo Magnifico had been a tyrant because he had paid himself out of the state coffers for the services he rendered the city; others might well have thought that he had neglected the family's banking business to devote himself to the greater glory of Florence and earned his pay.

During periods of acute stress, such as that of Machiavelli's employment in the chancellery, discussion turned more intensely to classical thinking about republican institutions, and during Machiavelli's lifetime with more sophistication than before. Florence was where political stress could have been expected to produce intelligent and original thought about politics.

It was the center of Renaissance intellectual life. Along with Milan, Venice, and the Papal States, it was one of the dominant powers in northern and central Italy; to the south, the Kingdom of Naples was fought over by the French and Spanish crowns. Florence was a great trading state, linked to the trade routes and commercial fairs of northern Europe, and prospering on a luxury trade in textiles in particular. It was the first banking center in Europe, and the Medici had prospered by being exceptionally skilled merchants and bankers. Its prominence now made Florence vulnerable, too powerful to be ignored, too weak to act as it chose.

The Florentine constitution was a classical city-state constitution. It had been instituted in 1293 after a revolt against the incumbent nobility. The aim was to ensure that neither the nobility nor the urban poor could hold unchecked power. The city was ruled by the *signoria*, a committee of eight "priors" chaired by the *gonfaloniere* of justice. It met together with two other committees—the committee of "twelve good men" and the committee of the sixteen *gonfalonieri* of the city's sixteen districts. Legislation was considered, but not initiated, by two other councils, the Council of the People and the Council of the Commune, whose members, three hundred and two hundred, respectively, were chosen by the *signoria*; under the Medici, they were replaced by the Seventy and the Hundred. These bodies rotated membership at very frequent intervals—two to six months—and the main committees of the republic were selected by lot. The names of eligible persons were placed in bags and the names of those who were to serve were drawn out. It was common for many names to be disqualified because the persons named were in arrears with their taxes or otherwise ineligible; this gave a lot of power to the scrutinizing committee that pronounced on eligibility to be considered and to serve. In a city of perhaps eighty thousand inhabitants in Machiavelli's day, some three thousand citizens each year were called on to perform a governmental function. It is easy to imagine that the unambitious who wished to attend to their families' affairs would hope to avoid public office if someone competent would take their place, while the ambitious would think it intolerable to be reduced to guessing whether their allies would be drawn from the bags. Upper-class families spent much time and energy ensuring that their allies were in the right place to protect their interests.

Such a complex and intrinsically slow-moving system was doomed to be overturned or subverted. For a long time it was subverted in ways that kept up appearances. In the sixty years before the republic of 1494, the Medici family did not hold prominent public offices. Yet nobody doubted that they ruled Florence. Their ascent to power was far from untroubled. Cosimo de'

Medici narrowly escaped death at the hands of the rival Albizzi family in 1433, when he was exiled for ten years and fined an enormous sum. The Albizzi instantly alienated their own supporters, and in 1434 Cosimo returned in triumph. He then ensured that the major bodies in the government were filled with his supporters. He achieved this partly within the constitution and partly without; an emergency council was assembled to reinstate him and remove his opponents, but he brought enough armed men to the meeting to secure his own safety and to ensure that the assembled citizens knew their duty. The Medici governed Florence within republican forms by controlling the personnel of government and ensuring that their friends were in control. The family suffered from hereditary uricemia, the disease underlying gout, and were short-lived, so their rule was never wholly secure. Because they died young, they inherited power young, and the success of any particular Medici ruler depended on temperament and innate capacity more than experience.

The two greatest Medici were Cosimo, who managed the affairs of Florence from 1434 to 1464, and Lorenzo the Magnificent, who took the reins in 1469 and died in 1492. Savonarola's Republic of Virtue came about partly because Lorenzo's successor, Piero di Lorenzo, was incompetent, but mostly for reasons outside anyone's control. In 1494 Lodovico Sforza of

Milan persuaded the French king, Charles VIII, to revive his claim to the Kingdom of Naples. To everyone's surprise, Charles took up the idea and headed into Italy. Florence had for fifty years played off the papacy, the empire, and France against each other to preserve its freedom of movement. Now, the game was up. The price of avoiding a full-scale invasion and the sack of Florence was allowing the French armies free passage down the west coast of Italy and accepting French occupation of the main cities en route. Piero became the scapegoat for this disaster and was sent packing.

From 1494 to 1498, the government was in the hands of the partisans of Girolamo Savonarola, an ascetic and visionary Dominican friar, but he could achieve no more than Piero in foreign affairs, and his campaign against ecclesiastical corruption drew the hostility of the papacy. Florence had always been friendly to the papacy; if Florence resiled from its allegiance, it was vulnerable to the depredations of warlords like Cesare Borgia operating from the Papal States. The city was also vulnerable to the threat of papal interdict, which the city would lie under if Savonarola was excommunicated. By withdrawing the church's protection from the persons and property of the citizens of Florence, the papacy could threaten the city's trade throughout Europe; the goods of the excommunicated were fair game. Papal pressure and Florentine discontent resulted in Savonarola's removal from office, followed by his torture and execution for heresy. The end of the affair was the establishment of the reconstituted republic of 1498, of which Machiavelli was the servant.

Its chief novelty was the creation of a Grand Council, in imitation of that in Venice. The motive was the wish to keep a tight rein on the *grandi* or *nobili* who might be tempted to seize power for themselves; it was also a last flicker of the Florentine urge to return to what were conceived of as the most ancient institutions of the city. The rules of membership resulted in a council far larger than anyone anticipated, and over the next fourteen years attempts were made to make this unwieldy body less useless when quick decisions were needed. Whether the republic could have survived its constitutional infirmities, given reasonable luck, is anyone's guess. It did not have reasonable luck; Italy was in a state of continual upheaval; French, Spanish, German, and Swiss armies fought sporadic wars across the country, and the Italian cities and princely states made and broke alliances in a futile attempt to gain advantage from the chaos. The papacy under Alexander VI and Julius II was well to the fore in this, and its fate was typical; they were strikingly successful in cementing the papacy's control of the Papal States, but fifteen years after the fall of the Florentine Republic, Rome was sacked by mutinous imperial armies, against the wishes of their commander in chief, Emperor Charles V. The humiliation of the Medici pope Clement VII provoked the expulsion of the Medici from Florence in the summer of 1527. The republic that followed lasted only until the final restoration of the Medici three years later and Florence's transformation into a grand duchy.

THE PRINCE

Machiavelli wrote *The Prince* following the failure of his beloved republic. What it is about is not hard to understand. The subject matter is one on which Machiavelli had often reflected during his career, as he watched Cesare Borgia imposing himself on cities whose government he had subverted, and as he contemplated the French conquest of Milan and the subsequent failure of the French to hang on to what they had taken. Machiavelli's topic is carefully specified: how a "new prince" is to take power and maintain himself in power. Nonetheless, although the topic is narrowly specified—Lorenzo de' Medici, to whom the book is dedicated, was preeminently a new prince to whose conduct chapter 5 of *The Prince* ("The Way to Govern Cities or Dominions That, Previous to Being Occupied, Lived under Their Own Laws") was all too glaringly relevant—the staying power of *The Prince* comes from its sweeping statements about human nature, the role of chance, or *fortuna*, in political life, and, above all, its insistence on the need for a clear-sighted appreciation of how men really *are* as distinct from the moralizing claptrap about how they *ought* to be that had brought so many princes and their states to ruin.

What made *The Prince* so timely emerges in the "Exhortation to Liberate Italy from the Barbarians," with which the book concludes. Lorenzo was the nephew of Pope Leo X; with the Medicis in power at Rome and in Florence, the way was open for the two most substantial powers in central Italy to pursue an ambitious military policy: "There is no one in whom Italy can now place any hope except your illustrious family which (because it is successful and talented, and favoured by God and the Church of which it is now head) can take the lead in saving her."[5]

The Prince divides in two; the first eleven chapters consider different sorts of principalities and the way to acquire and hold them; fourteen of the remaining fifteen form a parodic mirror of princes, covering a variety of topics familiar in the literature from Cicero and Seneca down to not yet written works like Castiglione's *The Courtier*: military prowess, honesty, mercy, generosity, the avoidance of contempt and hatred. It ends with an exhortation to the Medici princes to unify Italy and evict the "barbarians"—the foreign forces that had rampaged through Italy since 1494, and would continue to do so for another three decades. Italian writers in the nineteenth century hailed Machiavelli as the prophet of the *risorgimento*, but the description of the transalpine invaders as barbarians was common enough, even on the part of popes and dukes who had rashly invited them in to promote some local quarrel. It is an anachronism to see Machiavelli as a nineteenth-century Italian nationalist, rather than someone inspired by the glories of ancient Rome.

Machiavelli begins *The Prince* by telling Lorenzo that he has reflected both on his own experience and on ancient history to provide genuinely new advice. That in itself represented a double change in thinking, first in departing from the Florentine desire to revert to the past—which is a trait that perhaps reappears in the *Discourses*—and second in using ancient history not as a moral guide as in collections of *exempla* but as a quarry for examples of successful practice. *The Prince* then runs straight into serious business, beginning with laying out its subject matter: newly acquired principalities and their retention. The single paragraph that constitutes the entire opening chapter buries a wealth of recent history when it separates out hereditary states from states that are not, states that are completely new to a family from those annexed to a state that has long been ruled by the same family, states that were formerly republics from states that were principalities, and—a wide-ranging gesture that took in both the astonishing luck of Cesare Borgia and the reinsertion of the Medici with the assistance of Spanish troops—those "acquired either with the arms of others or with one's own, either through luck or favour or else through ability."[6]

Hereditary principalities are of no interest; they present no challenge to the political skills of the prince. Long habits of obedience give the incumbent an advantage over rivals; anyone who loses a state of which he is the hereditary ruler deserves to do so, though Machiavelli well knew that misfortune makes the inhabitants of any state turn against their rulers, hereditary or not. The crucial discussion begins with chapter 3, as he first turns to the way to keep control of "mixed" principalities, by which he means states that the prince has conquered with the aim of annexing them to his present state, explains why some states remain quiet when conquered while others do not, and embarks on the contrast between states acquired by the prince's own ability and those acquired with help from others.[7] The chaos of recent events dominates the discussion, but the Roman treatment of Greece during the conquest of the early second century BCE is adduced to emphasize the point he makes several times, that the French had bungled the acquisition of power in Italy when they first captured Milan and were then driven out.

The argument is simple: an annexed state will be hard to hold if its people are culturally very different from the conqueror's own state. The French would inevitably have a harder time securing their power in Milan than in, say, Burgundy, where the inhabitants lived much as in the rest of France and spoke more or less the same language as other Frenchmen. It is, however, not impossible to retain power under such conditions; the Romans were strikingly effective in keeping a grip on conquered kingdoms. The underlying difficulty is the same in all new acquisitions: it is not hard to acquire a state, because human beings are quick to be discontented, ready to blame their present rulers for their miseries, and happy to see the back of them. Having done so, they will discover that the new rulers are no improvement on their predecessors, and very likely worse, because the costs of conquest fall heavily on the conquered population. In that case, they will, if they can, rebel against their new masters.

What is to be done? Two things: first, ensure that there are no partisans of the deposed ruler to cause trouble; second, go and live in the conquered territories. Machiavelli did not by this literally mean that Louis XII should have gone in person to live in Milan, as the instances of Turkish and Roman conquest make clear. The thought is rather that he should have installed an administration of his own that could see what was going on and nip trouble in the bud. The French could have kept hold of Milan by establishing colonies, as the Romans would have done, or by installing their own administrators throughout the region, as the Turks do. "Colonies" in this context means settlements of soldiers who are rewarded with farms rather than colonization in the imperialist sense of the next several centuries. Doing neither, they were evicted. What startles modern readers is the calmness with which Machiavelli observes, "Wanting to annex territory is indeed very natural and normal, and when capable men undertake it, they are always praised, or at least not criticised. But if men who are not capable of achieving it are bent on undertaking it at all costs, this is a blunder that deserves censure."[8] This is the voice of Greek and Roman imperialism, adjusted to the world of the Renaissance. He argues that colonies of the Roman kind are better than an army of occupation because it is cheaper to establish colonies that can support themselves than to quarter soldiers on the country; moreover, because soldiers need so many resources, paying for them arouses great irritation. The republic that Machiavelli served ground to a standstill because incessant warfare required decisions on taxation to pay for it that could not be arrived at within the unwieldy constitution; it is easy to see how much feeling hides behind these calm observations on military budgets.

The Machiavelli who was a scandal to European morality emerges in passing. As between soldiers and colonists, he says, colonists cause less anger because the only people injured are those whose land is seized for the benefit of the colonists. Since they will be few and scattered about the countryside, they do not pose a formidable problem. He then produces the underlying principle that governs the discussion: "It should be observed here that men should either be caressed or crushed; because they can avenge slight injuries, but not those that are very severe. Hence any injury done to a man must be such that there is no need to fear his revenge."[9] To a modern eye the assumption that the small farmers and other inhabitants in the countryside can safely be discounted because they are unorganized and unable to defend themselves against the evils visited upon them by the invaders is repulsive. Machiavelli accepts the assumptions of the Romans when they took over the territory of their neighbors; no Roman worried for long about the violation of their neighbors' human rights.

On the way to offering advice to princes who have taken over a republic that may not be glad to receive them, Machiavelli offers a nice vignette of the way in which a country that is used to being governed as a despotism will be easy to retain even by the not very skilled. His example is the empire of Alexander the

Great. Alexander had no sooner conquered his empire than he died, sighing for new worlds to conquer, but because the subjects of Darius, king of Persia, were used to being governed in a centralized state, Alexander's heirs did not need to take extraordinary measures to preserve their power. He might have observed that Athens in contrast tried to recover its freedom and was defeated by the highly competent Antipater. In fact, he draws a contrast with the Roman experience in Gaul, where innumerable small, independent tribes had been used to liberty and did not take kindly to rule by outsiders. He expected the same would soon happen in France. Perhaps presciently in view of the wars that were to plague France in the second half of the sixteenth century, he observes that not only were Brittany and Burgundy recent enough acquisitions to remember their independence of the French crown, but the aristocracy in general was very local in its attachments and ready to revolt against a monarchy based in Paris if provoked. They are easy enough to manage if their existing way of life is not disturbed, but unlikely to acquiesce in any tighter control than that.[10]

A long tradition of genuine self-government poses problems for a new prince. In republics, "there is greater vitality, more hatred, and a stronger desire for revenge; they do not forget, indeed cannot forget, their lost liberties." That being so, there are three pieces of advice worth hewing to: a ruler should be prepared to live in the conquered state; he should utterly destroy all the old institutions; or he should leave as many as possible intact, so as to govern with the least irritation to old sentiments. Machiavelli draws his morals from the Romans and the Spartans: "The Spartans held Athens and Thebes by establishing oligarchies there; yet they eventually lost control of them. In order to hold Capua, Carthage and Numantia, the Romans destroyed them; and consequently never lost them." Initially, the Romans tried to emulate the Spartans in exercising only a loose suzerainty over Greece, but eventually had to destroy the Greek kingdoms to avoid incessant revolts. Polybius's picture of the Romans seducing their conquered subjects by offering them participation in the Roman state and its way of life is not directly contradicted, but where Polybius asked, "How did Rome acquire an empire whose peoples came to feel loyal to Rome?" Machiavelli poses a tougher question, "How does one ensure that a conquest will 'take'?" His answer boils down to the familiar binary opposition: kill or caress. Either show a respect for their institutions by governing behind the shield they provide and veil your authority; or stamp on opposition, exile or kill the previous elite, and make it clear that those who are not for you are as good as dead.

Although the first eleven chapters of *The Prince* constitute a unity, they are internally structured in an interesting fashion. Machiavelli was fascinated by the contrast between those who were astute and effective operators in the political world, and deserved congratulation, and those who were installed in power by the efforts of others or by simple good luck. *Fortuna*, or chance, is one of the most hotly debated of Machiavelli's terms, and we shall return to it. The role of chance in politics is obvious; and it is impossible not to feel that some political actors have had more than their share of good luck and others more than their share of bad. To observe that some people are thrust to prominence by chance is to say nothing startling. This understates Machiavelli's interest in the subject. Florence was superstitious almost as a matter of policy. An extravagant example soon after Machiavelli's death was that in 1527 the newly revived republic elected Christ as its king; more generally, the Florentines were unusually ready to believe that prayer and self-mortification would attract divine favor. Conversely, they seemed unable to deal with Cesare Borgia just because it seemed that fortune, along with his father, Pope Alexander VI, was on his side. Machiavelli was deeply hostile to anything that undermined the Florentines' ability to analyze the balance of forces they confronted.

He draws a crucial contrast between those who rely on their own political capacity—*virtù*—and those who rely on others or on luck. Plainly the first are less vulnerable to fortune's turning against them or to their allies' leaving them in the lurch. Cesare Borgia is a puzzle for this simple dichotomy, as we shall see. Those who display outstanding virtue and are therefore less dependent on fortune are the heroes one would expect, though the presence of Moses alongside Theseus, Cyrus, and Romulus may raise eyebrows, as Machiavelli admits. Machiavelli lets himself be distracted by his four heroes into a reflection on the fate of Savonarola that produces one of his best aphorisms. In the middle of his reflections on those who acquired a principality through their own arms, he says, "all armed prophets succeed, whereas unarmed ones fail." The figure of the armed prophet is a trope of twentieth-century political analysis. Machiavelli says, "If Moses, Cyrus, Theseus and Romulus had been unarmed, the new order which each of them established would not have been obeyed for very long. This is what happened in our own times to Fra' Girolamo Savonarola, who perished together with his new order as soon as the masses began to lose faith in him; and he lacked the means of keeping the support of those who had believed in him, as well as of making those who had never had any faith in him believe."[11] Behind Savonarola were innumerable prophetic figures who had frightened the authorities of their day but whose followers, with the exception of the militarily effective Hussites of Bohemia, lacked the capacity to overthrow their ungodly rulers.

The intellectual interest of these thoughts lies below the surface. Machiavelli had a strong sense that although there was much to be said in politics for a sudden, bold stroke, human beings were also creatures of habit, both good and bad, which argued for taking things slowly. The Florentines' ingratitude toward rulers who were devoted to the republic, but meeting with undeserved misfortune, was a long ingrained bad habit. Good habits need to be inculcated. The aid of religion was not to be scorned, nor its efficacy overestimated. Habits of obedience should be instilled by a mixture of fear and favor and backed up by whatever moral and spiritual resources came to hand; force mattered because once everyone could see that opposition was fatal, they would obey, and their beliefs would come into line with the habit of obedience. The *fact* of obedience would soon turn into a belief that they *ought* to obey. Most writers have tended to palliate the familiar fact that conquered populations come to subject themselves voluntarily in this fashion; Machiavelli did not. Force creates acceptance, reluctant at first, but willing in due course. Not to know this is to throw away the chance of success. The thought that if belief sustains authority, authority can reinforce the beliefs that then sustain it, is true enough; but it lacks the sharp edge that Machiavelli gives the observation. The fact that unarmed prophets invariably fail means that we may believe as firmly as we like that God is on our side, but it will do us no good if physical force is not on our side as well.

THE PUZZLE OF CESARE BORGIA

Cesare Borgia is a major figure both in *The Prince* and in the *Discourses*. He presents a problem for Machiavelli. Was he, or was he not, unduly reliant on luck? Was he a skillful practitioner of the arts that new princes should possess and brought down in the end by pure bad luck; or was his success due only to luck, and was he brought down by a failure to take the measures he should have taken to ensure that bad luck could not destroy him? Of course, admirers of Machiavelli's cynical style can relish his discussion of Cesare Borgia's rise to power simply as a literary tour de force. Cesare, the brother of Lucrezia the famous poisoner,[12] was the son of the future Borgia pope Alexander VI. He was made a cardinal in his teens, but when Alexander became pope, the possibility beckoned of advancement in the secular realm. He renounced his cardinal's hat and was appointed captain general of the papal armies. Alexander's intention was to bring the Papal States firmly under the papacy's control, to enhance his son's prestige and power, and beyond that to unify the Italian states under his leadership.

This was what Machiavelli urged on Leo X and Lorenzo de' Medici in the final chapter of *The Prince*, and the policy itself was not one he deplored. What he deplored was the fact that the papacy was too weak to implement it, but too powerful to allow any other state to do so.[13] Alexander dismissed the so-called papal vicars, the agents who administered the Papal States, and left Cesare to secure the Romagna, which he did with astonishing energy and success. What would have happened if events had favored him is hard to say, but Alexander was pope for only half a dozen years (1497–1503), and Cesare himself was at death's door with malaria at the very moment his father died. He could not influence the papal succession, and his attempts to get on good terms with Julius II, who loathed the Borgias, got nowhere. Cesare fled to Naples, but was arrested, exiled, and imprisoned in Spain; he was killed in battle soon after being released in 1507. The question his career posed for Machiavelli was whether there was anything more that Cesare could have done to secure his position. Machiavelli inclines toward the view that there was not; perhaps, but only perhaps, a more prudent or longsighted man might have thought ahead to the election of a new pope after the death of Alexander, but Machiavelli cannot find it in himself to complain.

Because of the way Machiavelli tells the story, Cesare Borgia comes across as an almost operatic villain; more seriously, he is presented as someone whose wickednesses were directed intelligently and efficiently to the end of making himself master of the Romagna. He was not gratuitously but tactically cruel. One piece of villainy that Machiavelli reports admiringly was Borgia's plot to ensure that the Orsini gave him and his father no trouble. Having persuaded the leading members of the clan that he was genuinely interested in reconciliation, he got them to a conference at Senigallia, seized them, and over the next four weeks had them strangled. Machiavelli treats the behavior of the Orsini and their friends as shockingly naïve; modern readers are likely to think that Borgia's behavior is repulsive, but it could be said on his side that the men he murdered were no strangers to the acquisition of power by murdering friends and relatives, let alone to disposing of sworn enemies.[14]

Borgia's most impressive coup de théâtre was the killing of the unfortunate Messer Remirro de Orco, an event that Machiavelli commented on admiringly in his dispatches and discusses in *The Prince*. The tale and the moral are simple. The Romagna was part of the papal patrimony, but had fallen into the hands of assorted small-time rulers who would today be called kleptocrats, whose only aim was to extract whatever they could from their wretched subjects. Borgia saw that any government that could keep the peace would be accepted, if it provided justice according to law and avoided outright banditry. The first step was to secure the peace. For this purpose, he installed Remirro de Orco, to whom he gave full power to suppress dissent and restore order. His chosen agent was effective, but his methods aroused resentment. Borgia took two steps to ensure that the resentment did not reach back to himself. The first was to establish a regular court, to which lawyers could take grievances. The second was to have Remirro de Orco arrested, "cut in two pieces," and placed in the main square at Cesena the day after Christmas together with an executioner's block and a knife. "This terrible spectacle left the people both satisfied and amazed."[15]

Understanding Machiavelli's project, which was not that of shocking the sensibilities of later ages, but reflecting on the difficulties of instituting political order, whether princely or republican, allows us to move onto terrain where a great deal of ink has been spilled. Machiavelli rounds off the discussion of the establishment of new principalities with a brief chapter on "ecclesiastical principalities." There is something unnerving about Machiavelli's account of the peculiarities of the Papal States. They are "sustained by ancient religious institutions, which have been sufficiently strong to maintain their rulers in office however they live and act. Only they have states and do not defend them, and subjects whom they do not trouble to govern. . . ."[16] That is to say, under successive popes the Papal States fell into the hands of the warring families who monopolized the College of Cardinals, and everything went to rack and ruin. "And their subjects, though not properly governed, do not worry about it; they cannot get rid of these rulers, nor even think about doing so. Only these principalities, then, are secure and success-ful."[17] To rub in the insult, Machiavelli then observes that since these states are governed by a higher power, there is nothing he can say about them.

Of course, there is, because he goes on to say that the model of a successful ruler is Alexander VI, Cesare's father. By guile and brute force, and the agency of his son, Alexander reestablished the papacy as a secular power to reckon with; this, thought Machiavelli, left his successor Julius II in a strong position to make the church the arbiter of the fate of Italy. Machiavelli was wrong; the monarchies of France and Spain were in a different league from the Italian states in their ability to assemble armies and keep them in the field for long campaigns. Julius II also suffered from Machiavelli's real vice, which was not a taste for wickedness for its own sake, but the belief that a deft operator could out-smart all his enemies all the time.

The second part of *The Prince* then turns into an ironic commentary on the traditional mirror of princes. Machiavelli's obsession was with military effectiveness on the one hand and the ability to form absolutely clear policy on the other. The doctrine that only the armed prophet succeeds is reinforced by reflecting on the failure of the Sforza family to keep itself in power by paying sufficient attention to military matters. "A ruler should have no other objective and no other concern, nor occupy himself with anything else except war and its methods and practices, for this pertains only to those who rule."[18] The injunction spills over into a departure from the usual advice to princes; handbooks for princes praised humane learning and taught the prince to interest himself in the social graces. Machiavelli says the only recreation the prince might usefully take up is hunting because it is a good way of learning how to read the lay of the land, and this is a valuable skill in a general. Humane letters are neither here nor there except for the acquisition of genuine historical knowledge; history provides a storehouse of great achievements to imitate, and a gallery of great men to emulate.

As to princely virtue, princes, says Machiavelli, are blamed only for shortcomings that bring about the destruction of the state. It is good to be loyal, generous, kindly, and the like, just as it is bad to be mean, lascivious, frivolous, and an unbeliever. All the same, the prince should not give much heed to his personal characteristics, save insofar as they lead him astray in matters of policy. This is a dig at Cicero's *De officiis*, though worse is to come. It may seem also to be a rejection of Aristotle's injunction that the ruler should practice self-control in the areas of sex and money. In fact, this is a topic on which Aristotle and Machiavelli are at one: concerned with the political consequences of unchastity, not unchastity as such. Seducing upper-class women creates enmities that undermine the ruler's position. It is worth remembering, however, how far Machiavelli shares the orthodox Christian pessimism about human nature. He is closer to Augustine than to Pico della Mirandola and his conviction that we might make ourselves cherubim. It is not obvious that his grim view of human nature is Christian in origin, but he believes in a version of original sin: "all men are by nature bad and will do all the evil they can." They must be disciplined by good laws, and if law has broken down, then by any means possible. Machiavelli did not have a surprising moral theory; he had a surprising readiness to confront head-on the fact that politics requires the willingness to get your hands dirty.

Then comes the advice that has so upset Machiavelli's readers, when Machiavelli analyzes the prince's *virtù*. The Machiavellian concept of *virtù* has been analyzed to death. That it does not mean "virtue" in the sense of the Christian virtues is obvious; what it does mean, less obvious. Usually, it means ability or almost any quality that makes for political success. These are reflections not on virtuous princes, as one would find in any number of pious writers, but on the qualities that make for effectiveness. *The Prince* is a reflection on the *virtù* of one man, the prince; the *Discourses* is a reflection on the *virtù* of a whole people—the Romans in particular, but also the Swiss and other citizens of successful states. The citizens of Athens and Sparta displayed *virtù*, though their obsession with confining the citizenship to the natives of their cities prevented them from achieving the glory that Rome did. Whether *virtù* is the same property in a prince and a whole people is much debated, but a plausible view is that it is formally the same property, but different in content. It is always defined in terms of the qualities that bring political success, and political success is closely linked to the achievement of glory. Whether it is the Roman people or the hoped-for savior of Italian independence in the early 1500s, political success is the goal; the polity to be established and maintained is not the same, but the enterprise is. Because the Roman people had to create and maintain a free government and did so *collectively*, the qualities they required were different from those a new prince needs. To take an obvious instance, Machiavelli never had a high opinion of the ordinary man's courage in the abstract.[19] Without good leadership and good training, the ordinary man is cowardly and incompetent, though with good leadership and training, he can display great courage and endurance. The prince, on the other hand, is ex hypothesi bold, ambitious, and ready to get himself killed in the attempt to seize power.

The sharpest contrast occurs with virtues such as honesty and loyalty. The people cannot act as an effective collectivity unless everyone treats everyone else with a high degree of honesty and mutual loyalty; these must be proper character traits and not easily turned on and turned off pragmatically. The new prince, in contrast, must be ready to change his colors at a moment's notice. He cannot afford to be so honest that he does not know how to deceive his rivals and murder them when he has the chance. Even those who are generally honest must be ready to be brutal. Machiavelli describes Hannibal's extreme cruelty, his *terribilità*, as part of his *virtù*. Given that most of us dislike behaving brutally or dishonestly, we might wonder whether political success is worth having at this price; indeed, we might wonder what constitutes political success in the first place. Can it really be defined in terms of wading in blood to a tyrant's throne?

Machiavelli leaves the reader to make up his own mind, but some of what he thinks is obvious enough, and the rest must be conjectural. The reward for successfully constructing a republic is freedom; citizens can live a civil life, a *vivere civile*, and enjoy their possessions and their liberties in peace. They will not be victimized by the rich, or invaded by foreigners, or ill treated without recourse to the law. It is possible that this is not wholly different from the ordinary person's rewards for a prince's success in securing and holding a principality. Sheldon Wolin's elegant description of Machiavelli as dealing in "an economy of violence"[20] catches the point nicely; the successful prince may get into power by unpleasant means, may maintain himself in power by unpleasant means, and may be a person whose moral character we do not care for. But he diminishes the amount of random, unpredictable, pointless violence and cruelty that we have to suffer. The prince's political reward is power. The attractions of power are not something Machiavelli troubles to analyze; true to his classical masters, he assumes that we want to exercise power and want not to have it exercised over us.

The thought that violence and treachery are a currency that politicians employ intelligently to avert their excessive and uncontrolled use catches something of Machiavelli's aims. However, his ultimate goal is one the modern world is less happy to avow as he does, other than in sporting contexts. This is the attainment of glory. If one asks why anyone would seek power in the way Machiavelli takes for granted—it is a question Machiavelli asks only in the context of observing that the unpredictability of fortune might make one wonder whether it is worth trying—the answer is that men seek glory. They want to leave a great name. Here there is a real difference in the achievements of a prince and a republic. In a principality glory is obtained by the prince; this is one reason why the romantic idea that the Renaissance saw the state as a work of art is not an inappropriate metaphor for the work of the prince. But the ordinary people are passive; they are the raw material of princely glory. In a republic the people themselves are the heroes and the achievers of glory. If *virtù* is the quality that achieves glory, it is thus both the same and different in the prince and the people; it is the same in being essentially instrumental, that is, the qualities that make for success and enable the possessors of these qualities to achieve glory through that success, and different inasmuch as different sorts of people under very different circumstances achieve glory in principalities and republics. Nor is it merely a matter of success; some highly successful rulers were mere tyrants. Agathocles, the tyrant of Syracuse, illuminates Machiavelli's view. He not only held power for a long period but drove the Carthaginians out of Sicily. But he had been freely elected by the citizens of Syracuse, and then made himself a tyrant, holding by force and treachery what he had been freely given. Needless cruelty and treachery are unforgivable.

Having laid the ground with his discussion of warfare and his scorn for the attainments of the courtier, Machiavelli launches into the characteristics of the successful prince. The most famous moment in the discussion comes in chapter 18, ominously entitled "How Rulers Should Keep Their Promises." The reader has by now been told that the prince should not *be* generous, though he should try to *appear* so, and has been reminded that it is better to be feared than to be loved—since people do not much mind revolting against the good-natured, but think twice about rebelling against the lethally severe—so it comes as no surprise that Machiavelli's advice is to keep faith only as and when it serves our ends. Honesty is a virtue and men are rightly praised for it, but a prince who is honest when he should not be makes himself a prey to his enemies. It is in this context that Machiavelli turns Cicero's advice on its head.

LIONS AND FOXES AND POLITICAL ETHICS

For Cicero the fact that even animals obey law in a certain sense—they are endowed by nature with habits useful to their survival—does not blur the distinction between man and beast. Men must obey a specifically human law; it teaches rational beings how to act for the common good. Human courage is not the lion's savagery; human intelligence is not the fox's cunning. To which Machiavelli replies, "Since a ruler, then, must know how to act like a beast, he should imitate both the fox and the lion, for the lion is liable to be trapped, whereas the fox cannot ward off wolves. One needs, then, to be a fox to recognise traps and a lion to frighten away wolves." Once more, the ruthless Alexander VI is praised for his duplicity: he "was concerned only with deceiving men; and he always found them gullible."[21]

One question must occur to the reader who reads Machiavelli in a friendly spirit. Setting aside the wickedness of rulers who follow his advice, can anyone act with quite the amoral verve and flair that Machiavelli advocates? Machiavelli takes the question seriously; but he circles around it, first asking how rulers can avoid being despised—mostly by being ferocious in repressing rivals and opponents—and then what they must do to gain a reputation. The discussion once more displays Machiavelli's taste for the spectacular; his hero is Ferdinand of Aragon, who united the Iberian Peninsula, drove out the Moors from their last strongholds, and, by a mixture of guile and military skill, first seized the Kingdom of Naples from its previous ruler with French assistance and then turned around and evicted the French. But Machiavelli admits that we cannot always be on top of events; often we have to cobble together a strategy in circumstances we would not have chosen. Then caution is better than rashness. The concession seems to be wrung from him. The sole point on which Machiavelli and the advice books coincide is the need to avoid flatterers. Like generations of political scientists after him, Machiavelli observes that princes have a hard time obtaining impartial advice, because people will tell them whatever they think the prince wants to hear. The remedy is to appoint to one's service people who are described in terms that sound very like a description of the former secretary of the Ten of War.

The Prince ends with a double peroration. The true peroration is, of course, the exhortation to liberate Italy from the barbarians. The pre-peroration is the engaging chapter on the role of fortune in human affairs. Short though *The Prince* is, one could be forgiven for thinking after a quick reading that being a Machiavellian hero is an exhausting and unprofitable activity; when there is peace, we must be active in making preparations for war; we should befriend the ordinary people, but not be too familiar with them, lest we become despised; we must watch out for our enemies and strike before they do, but we must not attend too carefully to the dangers of assassination, because only the incompetent or the oppressive run much risk. Steering a delicate path between an excess of caution and an overdose of rashness promises to be hard work, too.

Is the task hopeless? Machiavelli observes that it is a common view that "the affairs of the world are so much ruled by fortune and by God that the ability of men cannot control them." It is a view by which he is tempted, especially in view of the chaos that has gripped Italy for the previous two decades. Nonetheless, he refuses to agree that human freedom is of no account, and is "disposed to hold that fortune is the arbiter of half our actions, but that it lets us control roughly the other half."[22] It is interestingly unclear just what Machiavelli thinks. He sometimes suggests that all fortune amounts to is forces that we are commonly bad at controlling: "I compare fortune to one of those dangerous rivers that, when they become enraged flood the plains, destroy trees and buildings, move earth from one place and deposit it in another. . . . But this does not mean that when the river is not in flood, men are unable to take precautions, by means of dykes and dams, so that when it rises next time, it will either not overflow its banks, or if it does, its force will not be so uncontrolled or damaging."[23] That suggests the usual Machiavellian moral: men are chronically idle about taking precautions while things are going well. They are lulled into thinking that all will be well, because things are going well at present, and then something happens that they might have prevented but that they have foolishly taken no trouble to prevent. And as a result they are destroyed.

At other times fortune is represented as a real force for good or evil, even if it is not *wholly* outside our control even then. How well we do in a risky political enterprise is very much a matter of whether our style, temperament, characteristic mode of operation suits the conditions; sometimes the schemes of a cautious man will come adrift because the situation demands boldness, and sometimes the cautious man will succeed where the bold one does not. If—but it is very much the if of *per impossibile*—"it were possible to change one's character to suit the times and circumstances, one would always be successful."[24] Machiavelli then embarks on a set-piece on the character of Julius II. The Florentines found him entirely impossible to deal with; they could not deal with his rages, they could not predict his plans, and he himself may not quite have known what he was going to do next. But he was a bold military leader and during a very brief pontificate strikingly successful.

That, says Machiavelli, was because he was bold and impetuous, and the times suited him. Had he lived when a more cautious policy was required, he would have been undone because he could not possibly have acted otherwise than he did. All the same, says Machiavelli, in terms that cause our eyebrows to lift, "it is better to be impetuous than cautious, because fortune is a woman, and if you wish to control her, it is necessary to treat her roughly. And it is clear that she is more inclined to yield to men who are impetuous than to those who are calculating. Since fortune is a woman, she is always well disposed towards young men, because they are less cautious and more aggressive, and treat her more boldly."[25] How much more than a rhetorical flourish this may be, it is impossible to say. Machiavelli never suggested that he held distinctively un-Christian views; on the other hand, he never said anything to suggest deep piety. Since he cared a great deal about his literary skills, it might have been no more than decoration to make a point of some seriousness; on the other hand, it may have been something deeper than lip service to the idea that fate is an active force in the world, bringing us to good and evil on a whim. Polybius, after all, thought a lot about the reality of *tyche*, or fate, chance, fortune.

FROM *THE PRINCE* TO THE *DISCOURSES*

The Prince ends with an exhortation to Leo X to unite Italy and render the Medici forever glorious by expelling the barbarians from Italian soil. Machiavelli's hope is for Italy to recover its ancient Roman glory, and this theme connects *The Prince* and the *Discourses*. The *Dis-*

courses purports to be, and often really is, a commentary on Livy's *History of Rome*. It is broken into three books, of which the first is a sustained discussion of the principles underlying the creation and sustaining of a successful republic; the second focuses on the expansion of Rome, and the third on the importance of great leaders in the life of the Roman Republic. Writers on Machiavelli have some difficulty deciding whether it is astonishing that the *Discourses* is very different from *The Prince*, or whether it is the similarities in the two works that are really astonishing. Part of the answer is that the principles of statecraft that underlie both works are very much the same. Examples of useful ruthlessness often appear briefly in *The Prince* and are discussed at length in the *Discourses*; Cesare Borgia's exploits reinforce the lessons of the Romans; Julius II's impetuousness is praised; and the view of human nature in *The Prince* underpins Machiavelli's complaint in the *Discourses* that even men of the vilest character do not know how to be thoroughgoing in their wickedness and flinch just when they ought to go to extremes.[26]

Although the principles of statecraft and the underlying view of human nature are the same, the occasion and the purpose of the discussion are very different. Republics are not principalities—here thought of as states ruled as if they are the personal possession of a prince—and the focus of the *Discourses* is the creation of a self-sustaining constitutional order in a republic. The model is Polybius. Machiavelli held many views that readers of Polybius would find familiar, and he confronted the same puzzle about Rome's success in reforming its constitutional arrangements by trial and error. The body politic is rightly thought of as like the human body. It is usually essential to be born healthy, since just as a sickly child may, with luck and care, survive a long time, but never do much, so an ill-constructed state will never amount to much on the world stage. But Rome interests Machiavelli in the sixteenth century as it had Polybius and Cicero long before, because it violates that maxim. It went through several constitutional upheavals in its early years when it threw out its kings and adopted a republican constitution, and again when the secession of the plebs forced the ruling elite to open public offices to the non-aristocracy. If it is harder to rebuild one's boat in midocean than to make it watertight before leaving shore, the Romans show that some people have the talent, energy, and good luck to get away with rebuilding on the voyage.

Writers on Machiavelli have debated at length what he thought he was claiming for himself when he claimed that in writing the *Discourses* he was traveling "a new route."[27] He says that he is using historical evidence properly, a thing that "the proud indolence" of these Christian states prevents Italian rulers from doing. It is not clear who these indolent princes are, nor what he thinks distinguishes his use of history from that of previous writers. To the extent that he commits himself to any principle more profound than a contempt for anyone who confuses analysis with moralizing, he echoes Thucydides. Human nature is the same at all times and places, so whatever has happened in the past can be emulated if worth emulating or avoided if it should be avoided. He comments on the absurdity of contemporary aristocrats and rich men who dig up antique statues and have modern copies made of them, but who do not see how much more valuable it would be to understand the actions and ideas of great political and military leaders of the ancient world and learn how to copy them. Indeed, his great complaint appears to be that the majority of those who read history "take pleasure in the variety of events which history relates, without ever thinking of imitating the noble actions, deeming that not only difficult but impossible, as though heaven, the sun, the elements, and men had changed their motions and power, and were different from what they were in ancient times."[28] Machiavelli is not a writer who excites the desire to carp, but his reliance on the uniformity of human nature to underpin what one might describe as the method of "look, analyze, copy" seems on its face to consort badly with his recognition that circumstances change and that we had better change with them. The one thing for which we ought not to reproach him is a failure to appreciate that the cultural, religious, and social *milieu* of the ancient world was too unlike that of Renaissance Italy for "look, analyze, copy" to work. Social thinkers in the nineteenth century ascribed many of the disasters of the French Revolution to the sheer impossibility that eighteenth-century Parisians should be like Romans of the third century BCE. It is not obvious that the complaint has the same force in an Italian city-state three centuries earlier.

Machiavelli's detachment from conventional moralizing has tempted commentators to think that the novelty is that Machiavelli set out to practice what later ages would recognize as political science, an inductively based comparative inquiry into what methods work where, when, and how. This is wholly implausible. Apart from Machiavelli's toleration of internal contradiction, as when he says at one point that Rome was poor and at another that Rome was rich, there is nothing to suggest he had such a conception of science. It would have been surprising if he had, since it would have antedated the scientific self-consciousness of natural scientists themselves by two centuries. Other commentators have made much of his seeming endorsement of the cyclical theory of history that appears in Plato's *Republic* and was borrowed for his own purposes by Polybius.

The *Discourses* is certainly Polybian at the level of style and intellectual concerns, even though Polybius was reflecting on events in his own lifetime whereas Machiavelli is commenting on Livy's account of the foundation and growth of the early republic. Polybius's historical style, and the pleasure he takes in men's securing their ends by deft acts of deceit is very like Machiavelli's; nonetheless, the so-called cyclical theory of history is neither a theory nor very cyclical. What it offers Machiavelli is reinforcement for his conviction that the wheel of fate turns unpredictably. Princes of sufficient flair and republics with good laws allied to good arms can master necessity for a time, but the historical judgment to which Machiavelli is most attached is that success breeds failure, because in the end the imperial republic is corrupted by wealth. And like Polybius, Machiavelli leaves the reader unsure whether chance, *tyche*, or *fortuna* is an active force in history.

Machiavelli does what he does in *The Prince*, which is offer prudential maxims illustrated and defended by appeal to historical events. Machiavelli's reputation as a "teacher of evil" rested on *The Prince*, but his insistence that when the means accuse, the end must excuse is every bit as prominent in the *Discourses*, which is indeed where the aphorism comes from. Machiavelli adopts what would be an uncompromisingly republican standpoint, except that it is *either* republics *or* kingdoms that men are praised for founding; what is indefensible is the institution of a tyranny. How far that conflicts with *The Prince* is an open question; there Machiavelli seems almost to take the view that Hobbes later made famous, that tyranny is but "monarchy misliked." It seems that he thought it perfectly proper to adopt dictatorial methods in emergency as the Romans did, but perfectly intolerable to establish an enduring tyranny. That, after all, is the moral of his defense of Romulus's actions in slaying Remus; one must do whatever it takes to get a political society up and running, but the tyrant is the enemy of his people, is rightly killed by whoever can do it, and is the polar opposite of the lawful ruler. Machiavelli's views on tyranny are conventional in the classical tradition, but decidedly non-Pauline.

For all that, he is committed to the view that only autocrats can institute or restore a state. There must be a founding moment when the new order is laid down, just as there must be a similar moment if a state is rescued by being returned to its first principles in a revolutionary reconstitution. Moses, Romulus, and Theseus are the heroes of both *The Prince* and the *Discourses*. But the emphasis in the *Discourses* falls on what Machiavelli describes as *ordini*, which is not rendered absolutely faithfully as "laws"; much as Rousseau does later, when he appears to distinguish between the fundamental laws of a political system and "decrees," so Machiavelli seems to have in mind something very like the laws that define the constitutional order. It is an idea with which states with written constitutions are wholly familiar, and indeed the constitution of Germany today is called the "Basic Law." Beginnings are very different from sustainings; the irregular, often violent, and improvised actions of the founder hero must be succeeded by the regular election of leaders according to law.

The element that is hardly touched on in *The Prince* but is very prominent in the *Discourses* is religion. The Romans are praised for taking religion both seriously and unseriously. They took religion seriously in the sense that they understood the importance of religion as social cement. It is a useful aid to public morality; it urges courage in battle; it reinforces the respect for ancestors and affection for children on which solidarity across generations depends. Christianity is on the whole ill suited for such purposes; being otherworldly, it takes people's minds off their political and military duties and makes them attend only to their own salvation. It is a milk and water religion, urging its adherents to turn the other cheek. The Romans were not known for turning the other cheek. Educated Romans did not take religion seriously as a matter of metaphysics; metaphysics was for philosophers, not for the man in the street, let alone for the legionary. A relaxed view of the truth of religion allowed the leaders of Roman society to manipulate the practices and rituals of Roman religious observance as they needed. It was wise to ensure that the auguries before battle predicted success, and a competent commander would know how to do it. However, it was also essential that common soldiers treated the auguries with respect and that anyone who insulted them was promptly executed.

Machiavelli's animus is directed at the institution of the papacy rather than at Christianity or at other non-pagan religions. Chapter 12 of the *Discourses* is entitled "The Importance of Giving Religion a Prominent Influence in a State; and How Italy Was Ruined Because She Failed in This Respect through the Influence of the Church of Rome."[29] Early Christianity could have provided the basis for social cohesion, loyalty, good morals, and public spirit; but early sixteenth-century Italy shows what happens if there is an institution in the midst of society that is both corrupt considered as a religious institution—which sickens all of what passes for religion, and makes them irreligious—and inept as a political institution—one that has lost its grip on its possessions and has invited foreign powers into Italy, to the detriment both of its own subjects and those of all the other Italian states. It is observations such as these that got Machiavelli's works onto the Index.

Three further doctrines of the *Discourses* bear examination, since they had a considerable impact on republican thought and are by no means a reworking of commonplaces. One is Machiavelli's claim that a certain amount of uproar in a republic is conducive to liberty. There seems to be no prior defense of this proposition, and it is at odds with the entire tendency of Christian thinking, with its emphasis on harmony; it is at odds also with the utopian tradition running back to Plato's *Republic* and with all previous republican thinking. It must certainly be true that all defenders of mixed constitutions rely on the common people, or whatever proportion of them they include in "the people," to stand up for their own political rights; if they did not do so, they could not fulfill their role in the system of checks and balances. All classical writers—Aristotle, Polybius, and Cicero among them—took it for granted that they would do so, and were less afraid that they might be too passive than that they would get out of hand. Machiavelli's doctrine is perfectly clear, and offered as a novelty. The secession of the plebeians forced the ruling elite to take seriously the fact that the lower classes fed the city and kept the elite clothed and housed; it encouraged the lower classes to insist on their rights and privileges in the Roman state. It therefore gave notice to those who might oppress them that they would not stand for it, and so preserved liberty.[30] Indeed, continued class conflict and the permanent tension between the upper and lower classes made Rome both powerful and free. We need not accept this rosy view of the freedom available to the Roman lower classes to see the point; it was made by Edmund Burke and many others long afterward. It was shocking to Machiavelli's contemporaries, who thought that endorsing the usefulness of uproar was, in the conditions of early sixteenth-century Italy, much like pouring oil on a raging fire; had they looked north to Reformation Germany, they might have taken an equally cool view about the virtues of disputatiousness.

A second idea that makes a reappearance in republican writers thereafter is Machiavelli's defense of the popular republic against the aristocratic republic. The argument is intricately wound in with another about the merits of a republic designed for longevity as against one designed for increase. The Roman Republic was an expansive republic, and Machiavelli admired it for that reason. Even though Venice had acquired a maritime empire in the Adriatic and beyond, and substantial territories in the terra firma, it was a republic designed for longevity. Machiavelli's passion for a state that cut a great figure on the stage of world events led him to side with Rome against Venice. The defense of a popular rather than an aristocratic republic is not an argument in favor of the institutions of Rome in particular, but a defense of Florentine populism against Venetian narrowness. The argument runs thus: republics are endangered by "gentlemen"—there are many synonyms, such as *nobili* or *grandi*—who are defined by Machiavelli not simply as men who are rich or wellborn but as those with the vices of feudal landowners. These vices, as in More's *Utopia*, center on their keeping large numbers of retainers who are a threat to the peace both when they are employed to further the political ambitions of their masters and when they have been dismissed from his service and know no way to make a living save banditry. It is the ability of the *grandi* and *nobili* to raise private armies and subvert the state that alarms him; on this matter he and Cicero would speak with one voice.

Venice seemed to be a puzzle because it was aristocratic but had not been ruined by the ruling aristocracy. Venice practiced *guberno stretto*, a "narrow" regime in which eligibility for office was confined to the descendants of those who had been eligible when the Great Council was "closed" in 1297, at the end of a long series of earlier reforms; it was an aristocratic republic, managed by a narrow oligarchy. Florence had adopted *guberno largo*, a "wide" regime, to keep the aristocrats in check and ensure that decisions on taxation and other important matters were made by a wider rather than a smaller body of citizens. In abolishing the Great Council on their return in 1512 and physically destroying the hall in which it met, the Medici were announcing that they would govern as de facto princes behind a republican screen, and that the screen would be an aristocratic rather than a popular republic. Machiavelli's puzzle was to explain why Venice had not been ruined by its gentlemen. His answer was that they were not gentlemen except in name. They were rich merchants whose wealth was in money and goods. As long as traders remain traders, they pose no threat to the republic. They cannot prosper by reducing their fellow citizens to servitude, and they have no interest in maintaining private armies on the landed estates that ex hypothesi they do not have. Later political sociologists agreed.

Finally, then, the fatal question and the third of Machiavelli's surprising thoughts. Like Polybius, Machiavelli thinks that success cannot endure indefinitely, and like Hume after him, he thinks the works of man are destined to decay, no matter what. Within a dozen pages of the end of the *Discourses*, Machiavelli is still insisting that if "on the decision to be taken wholly depends the safety of one's country, no attention should be paid either to justice or to injustice, to kindness or to cruelty, or to its being praiseworthy or ignominious. On the contrary, every other consideration being set aside, that alternative should be wholeheartedly adopted which will save the life and preserve the freedom of one's country."[31] Over and over, he insists that half measures always lead to ruin, that boldness often achieves what caution cannot, as though the cultivation of

Roman dash and vigor will carry everything before it. Yet he also says that success is self-defeating, that no republic can last forever, that corruption will always attend the achievement of great things.

A successful republic will acquire more territory, incorporate more citizens, become prosperous. When it becomes prosperous, people will begin to turn in on themselves and think about their own wealth rather than the good of the republic. The martial virtues will decline, and taste for soft living will creep in. Mercenaries will be hired to replace citizen-soldiers. The very rich will think how they can turn their wealth into power, and so subvert the republic. The ordinary people will remain uncorrupted longer than their betters, but they, too, can be suborned and turned into willing accomplices of the men who offer them a share of the loot or an exemption from the demands of the republic. Then there will be the decline and fall that the Roman Republic went through. A strong man lives longer than an unhealthy one, but both die in the end; and so it is with states. Readers' reactions to Machiavelli depend heavily on their reactions to such banal, but important, truths about human existence. It is clear that Machiavelli thought that life was for the living and that death was its inevitable companion; and by the same token that the world of politics had its own raison d'être, which only the fainthearted or slow-footed would fail to be moved by. Those who were neither fainthearted nor slow-footed but who marched to a different drummer could always retire to a monastery and contemplate eternal verities. It does not seem that Machiavelli would have condemned them for so doing; but he had nothing to say to them.

NOTES

1. Niccolò Machiavelli, letter to Francesco Vettori, December 10, 1513, in *The Prince*, trans. Quentin Skinner and Russell Price (Cambridge: Cambridge University Press, 1988), p. 93.

2. J. H. Burns and Mark Goldie, eds., *Cambridge History of Political Thought, 1450–1700* (Cambridge: Cambridge University Press, 1991), pp. 55–56.

3. Niccolò Machiavelli, *Discourses on Livy* (I.9), ed. Max Lerner (New York: Random House, 1950), pp. 138–39.

4. Machiavelli, "Dedicatory Letter," in *The Prince*, pp. 3–4.

5. Machiavelli, *The Prince*, p. 88.

6. Ibid., p. 5.

7. Ibid., pp. 6–14.

8. Ibid., p. 13.

9. Ibid., p. 9.

10. Comparing ibid., pp. 8 and 16.

11. Ibid., p. 21.

12. Who makes a cameo appearance in Max Beerbohm's wonderful spoof "'Savonarola' Brown" in *Seven Men* (Harmondsworth: Penguin, 1954).

13. Machiavelli, *Discourses* (I.12), p. 152.

14. Machiavelli, *The Prince*, p. 25.

15. Ibid., p. 26.

16. Ibid., pp. 39–40.

17. Ibid., p. 40.

18. Ibid., pp. 51–52.

19. Machiavelli, *Discourses* (I.57), pp. 258ff.

20. Sheldon S. Wolin, *Politics and Vision: Continuity and Innovation in Western Political Thought* (Princeton: Princeton University Press, 2004), pp. 197–99.

21. Machiavelli, *The Prince*, pp. 61–62.

22. Ibid., pp. 84–85.

23. Ibid., p. 85.

24. Ibid., p. 86.

25. Ibid., p. 87.

26. Machiavelli, *Discourses* (I.27), pp. 185–86.

27. Ibid., introduction, pp. 103–5.

28. Ibid., p. 105.

29. Ibid., pp. 149–53.

30. Ibid. (I.4), pp. 118–20.

31. Ibid. (3.41), p. 528.

Selections

A NOTE ON THE SELECTIONS

THE SELECTIONS FROM MACHIAVELLI'S writings that follow reflect the discussion of Machiavelli's political ideas above, and not the full range of Machiavelli's interests. Because *The Prince* is a very short work, I have included a substantial part of it, for the most part omitting only the historical examples that Machiavelli employed to back up his advice. His *Discourses*, on the other hand, are very substantial and full of elaborate historical examples; I have contented myself with extracting discussions of the general principles of statecraft most relevant to the argument of *The Prince*. Among Machiavelli's works not represented here, his history of Florence and his discussion of warfare are the most relevant; but anyone curious about Machiavelli's broader literary tastes will enjoy his play *Mandragola*—"Mandrake"—

that he wrote for his former colleague Francesco Guicciardini. It features Nicia, an elderly husband desperate for an heir; Lucrezia, his young wife; Callimaco her would-be lover; Lucrezia's mother; a marriage broker; and the rascally friar Timoteo. Disguised as a doctor, Callimaco urges Nicia to give his wife a drug made from the root of the Mandrake, telling him it will make her fertile, but kill the first man she has intercourse with; Lucrezia is reluctant, but gives in to the urging of her mother and Friar Timoteo. Callimaco is then passed off as a young man whom the friar has tricked into sleeping with Lucrezia. All ends happily: Callimaco reveals the hoax in the morning; Lucrezia concludes that her adultery was divinely ordained and takes Callimaco as her permanent lover. The friar and the marriage broker pocket their earnings. Nicia will get his heir. One might think the play would offend the devout, but Guicciardini was the loyal servant of the Medici popes Leo X and Clement VII at the very highest levels. If the relish for well-judged deception that runs through *The Prince* is evident in *Mandragola*, it is doubtful that Machiavelli meant to do more than poke fun at some stock characters—gullible husbands, errant wives, and greedy friars among them.

NICCOLÒ MACHIAVELLI TO FRANCESCO
VETTORI, THEN FLORENTINE ENVOY TO
THE HOLY SEE, 10 DECEMBER 1513

When evening comes, I return home and enter my study; before I go in I remove my everyday clothes, which are very muddy and soiled, and put on clothes that are fit for a royal court. Being thus properly clad, I enter the ancient courts of the men of old, in which I am received affectionately by them and partake of the food that properly belongs to me, and for which I was born. There I do not hesitate to converse with them, and ask them why they acted as they did; and out of kindness they respond. For four hours I experience no boredom, I forget all my troubles and my fear of poverty, and death holds no more terrors for me: I am completely absorbed in them.

Since Dante says that there can be no real knowledge if what has been learned is not retained, I have written down what has been valuable in their conversations, and have composed a little book *On Principalities*, in which I delve as deeply as I can into this subject, and discuss what a principality is, how many different types there are, how they are gained, how they are held, and why they are lost. And if any of my pieces have ever pleased you, this one should be to your taste. Moreover, it should be welcome to a ruler, especially to a new one. Accordingly, I am dedicating it to His Magnificence Giuliano. Filippo Casavecchia has seen it; he could tell you something about the work itself, and the discussions I have had with him about it, even though I am still revising and adding to it.

Honoured Ambassador, you want me to abandon this life and come to enjoy life with you. I shall certainly do so, but at present I am engaged with certain matters; however, in about six weeks they should be resolved. What makes me hesitate is that the Soderini are there, and if I went there I should be obliged to visit them and speak with them. I am afraid that on my return I would not dismount at home but at the Bargiello. For although this regime is very solidly based and is very stable, it is still new and therefore suspicious. Moreover, there are plenty of know-alls (like Pagolo Bertini) who, so as to be thought clever, would act in a way that might get me into trouble. I hope that you will be able to allay these fears; if so, I shall certainly come to see you during the period I have indicated.

I have discussed this little work of mine with Filippo, and also whether it is a good idea to present it or not; and if so, whether I should take it personally or send it instead. One reason for not presenting it is my fear that Giuliano might not read it, and then that Ardinghelli might appropriate for himself any credit arising from this latest labour of mine. An argument for presenting it is that I am pressed by need, for I find myself in difficulties, and if my present condition persists for very long my poverty will make me despised; there is also my desire that these Medici rulers should begin to use me, even if they should start by making me roll a stone. If I did not then win them over, I should have only myself to blame. This work, if they should read it, will reveal that I have not been asleep or wasted my time during the fifteen years that I have been engaged in studying statecraft. And anyone should very much want to be served by a man who is very knowledgeable through profiting from the experiences of others. Moreover, no doubts should be cast on my trustworthiness because, since I have always been trustworthy, I could not now be prepared to become untrustworthy. For anyone who has been trustworthy and disinterested for forty-three years, as I have, cannot change his character. And my very poverty testifies to my fidelity and disinterestedness. I should be glad, then, if you would write to me, giving your views on this subject. I commend myself to you. May you flourish.

10 December 1513
Niccolò Machiavelli in Florence

THE PRINCE

Translated from the Italian by Luigi Ricci
Revised by E. R. P. Vincent

NICCOLÓ MACHIAVELLI
TO
LORENZO THE MAGNIFICENT
SON OF PIERO DI MEDICI

It is customary for those who wish to gain the favour of a prince to endeavour to do so by offering him gifts of those things which they hold most precious, or in which they know him to take especial delight. In this way princes are often presented with horses, arms, cloth of gold, gems, and such-like ornaments worthy of their grandeur. In my desire, however, to offer to Your Highness some humble testimony of my devotion, I have been unable to find among my possessions anything which I hold so dear or esteem so highly as that knowledge of the deeds of great men which I have acquired through a long experience of modern events and a constant study of the past.

With the utmost diligence I have long pondered and scrutinised the actions of the great, and now I offer the results to Your Highness within the compass of a small volume: and although I deem this work unworthy of

Your Highness's acceptance, yet my confidence in your humanity assures me that you will receive it with favour, knowing that it is not in my power to offer you a greater gift than that of enabling you to understand in a very short time all those things which I have learnt at the cost of privation and danger in the course of many years. I have not sought to adorn my work with long phrases or high-sounding words or any of those superficial attractions and ornaments with which many writers seek to embellish their material, as I desire no honour for my work but such as the novelty and gravity of its subject may justly deserve. Nor will it, I trust, be deemed presumptuous on the part of a man of humble and obscure condition to attempt to discuss and direct the government of princes; for in the same way that landscape painters station themselves in the valleys in order to draw mountains or high ground, and ascend an eminence in order to get a good view of the plains, so it is necessary to be a prince to know thoroughly the nature of the people, and one of the populace to know the nature of the nature of princes. . . .

Chapter II

OF HEREDITARY MONARCHIES

I will not here speak of republics, having already treated of them fully in another place. I will deal only with monarchies, and will discuss how the various kinds described above can be governed and maintained. In the first place, the difficulty of maintaining hereditary states accustomed to a reigning family is far less than in new monarchies; for it is sufficient not to transgress ancestral usages, and to adapt one's self to unforeseen circumstances; in this way such a prince, if of ordinary assiduity, will always be able to maintain his position, unless some very exceptional and excessive force deprives him of it; and even if he be thus deprived, on the slightest mischance happening to the new occupier, he will be able to regain it.

We have in Italy the example of the Duke of Ferrara, who was able to withstand the assaults of the Venetians in 1484 and of Pope Julius in 1510, for no other reason than because of the antiquity of his family in that dominion. In as much as the legitimate prince has less cause and less necessity to give offence, it is only natural that he should be more loved; and, if no extraordinary vices make him hated, it is only reasonable for his subjects to be naturally attached to him, the memories and causes of innovations being forgotten in the long period over which his rule has extended; whereas one change always leaves the way prepared for the introduction of another.

Chapter III

OF MIXED MONARCHIES

But it is in the new monarchy that difficulties really exist. First, if it is not entirely new, but a member as it were of a mixed state, its disorders spring at first from a natural difficulty which exists in all new dominions, because men change masters willingly, hoping to better themselves; and this belief makes them take arms against their rulers, in which they are deceived, as experience later proves that they have gone from bad to worse. This is the result of another very natural cause, which is the inevitable harm inflicted on those over whom the prince obtains dominion, both by his soldiers and by an infinite number of other injuries caused by his occupation.

Thus you find enemies in all those whom you have injured by occupying that dominion, and you cannot maintain the friendship of those who have helped you to obtain this possession, as you will not be able to fulfil their expectations, nor can you use strong measures with them, being under an obligation to them; for which reason, however strong your armies may be, you will always need the favour of the inhabitants to take possession of a province. It was from these causes that Louis XII of France, though able to occupy Milan without trouble, immediately lost it, and the forces of Ludovico alone were sufficient to take it from him the first time, for the inhabitants who had willingly opened their gates to him, finding themselves deluded in the hopes they had cherished and not obtaining those benefits they had anticipated, could not bear the vexatious rule of their new prince. . . .

Chapter IV

WHY THE KINGDOM OF DARIUS, OCCUPIED
BY ALEXANDER, DID NOT REBEL AGAINST THE
SUCCESSORS OF THE LATTER AFTER HIS DEATH

Considering the difficulties there are in holding a newly acquired state, some may wonder how it came to pass that Alexander the Great became master of Asia in a few years, and had hardly occupied it when he died, from which it might be supposed that the whole state would have rebelled. However, his successors maintained themselves in possession, and had no further difficulties in doing so than those which arose among themselves from their own ambitions.

I reply that the kingdoms known to history have been governed in two ways: either by a prince and his servants, who, as ministers by his grace and permission, assist in governing the realm; or by a prince and by barons, who hold their positions not by favour of the ruler but by antiquity of blood. Such barons have states and subjects of their own, who recognise them as their lords, and are naturally attached to them. In those states which are governed by a prince and his servants, the prince possesses more authority, because there is no one in the state regarded as a superior other than himself, and if others are obeyed it is merely as ministers and officials of the prince, and no one regards them with any special affection.

Examples of these two kinds of government in our own time are those of the Turk and the King of France. All the Turkish monarchy is governed by one ruler, the others are his servants, and dividing his kingdom into "sangiacates," he sends to them various administrators, and changes or recalls them at his pleasure. But the King of France is surrounded by a large number of ancient nobles, recognised as such by their subjects, and loved by them; they have their prerogatives, of which the king cannot deprive them without danger to himself. Whoever now considers these two states will see that it would be difficult to acquire the state of the Turk; but having conquered it, it would be very easy to hold it. In many respects, on the other hand, it would be easier to conquer the kingdom of France, but there would be great difficulty in holding it. . . .

Chapter V
THE WAY TO GOVERN CITIES OR DOMINIONS THAT,
PREVIOUS TO BEING OCCUPIED, LIVED UNDER
THEIR OWN LAWS

When those states which have been acquired are accustomed to live at liberty under their own laws, there are three ways of holding them. The first is to despoil them; the second is to go and live there in person; the third is to allow them to live under their own laws, taking tribute of them, and creating within the country a government composed of a few who will keep it friendly to you. Because this government, being created by the prince, knows that it cannot exist without his friendship and protection, and will do all it can to keep them. What is more, a city used to liberty can be more easily held by means of its citizens than in any other way, if you wish to preserve it.

There is the example of the Spartans and the Romans. The Spartans held Athens and Thebes by creating within them a government of a few; nevertheless they lost them. The Romans, in order to hold Capua, Carthage, and Numantia, ravaged them, but did not lose them. They wanted to hold Greece in almost the same way as the Spartans held it, leaving it free and under its own laws, but they did not succeed; so that they were compelled to lay waste many cities in that province in order to keep it, because in truth there is no sure method of holding them except by despoiling them. And whoever becomes the ruler of a free city and does not destroy it, can expect to be destroyed by it, for it can always find a motive for rebellion in the name of liberty and of its ancient usages, which are forgotten neither by lapse of time nor by benefits received; and whatever one does or provides, so long as the inhabitants are not separated or dispersed, they do not forget that name and those usages, but appeal to them at once in every emergency, as did Pisa after being so many years held in servitude by the Florentines. But when cities or provinces have been accustomed to live under a prince, and the family of that prince is extinguished, being on the one hand used to obey, and on the other not having their old prince, they cannot unite in choosing one from among themselves, and they do not know how to live in freedom, so that they are slower to take arms, and a prince can win them over with greater facility and establish himself securely. But in republics there is greater life, greater hatred, and more desire for vengeance; they do not and cannot cast aside the memory of their ancient liberty, so that the surest way is either to lay them waste or reside in them.

Chapter VI

OF NEW DOMINIONS WHICH HAVE BEEN ACQUIRED
BY ONE'S OWN ARMS AND ABILITY

Let no one marvel if in speaking of new dominions both as to prince and state, I bring forward very exalted instances, for men walk almost always in the paths trodden by others, proceeding in their actions by imitation. Not being always able to follow others exactly, nor attain to the excellence of those he imitates, a prudent man should always follow in the path trodden by great men and imitate those who are most excellent, so that if he does not attain to their greatness, at any rate he will get some tinge of it. He will do as prudent archers, who when the place they wish to hit is too far off, knowing how far their bow will carry, aim at a spot much higher than the one they wish to hit, not in order to reach this height with their arrow, but by help of this high aim to hit the spot they wish to.

I say then that in new dominions, where there is a new prince, it is more or less easy to hold them according to the greater or lesser ability of him who acquires them. And as the fact of a private individual becoming a prince presupposes either great ability or good fortune, it would appear that either of these things would in part mitigate many difficulties. Nevertheless those who have been less beholden to good fortune have maintained themselves best. The matter is also facilitated by the prince being obliged to reside personally in his territory, having no others. But to come to those who have become princes through their own merits and not by fortune, I regard as the greatest, Moses, Cyrus, Romulus, Theseus, and their like. And although one should not speak of Moses, he having merely carried out what was ordered him by God, still he deserves admiration, if only for that grace which made him worthy to speak with God. But regarding Cyrus and others who have acquired or founded kingdoms, they will all be found worthy of admiration; and if their particular actions and methods are examined they will not appear very different from those of Moses, although he had so great a Master. And in examining their life and deeds it will be seen that they owed nothing to fortune but the opportunity which gave them matter to be shaped into what form they thought fit; and without that opportunity their powers would have been wasted, and without their powers the opportunity would have come in vain.

It was thus necessary that Moses should find the people of Israel slaves in Egypt and oppressed by the Egyptians, so that they were disposed to follow him in order to escape from their servitude. It was necessary that Romulus should be unable to remain in Alba, and should have been exposed at his birth, in order that he might become King of Rome and founder of that nation. It was necessary that Cyrus should find the Persians discontented with the empire of the Medes, and the Medes weak and effeminate through long peace. Theseus could not have shown his abilities if he had not found the Athenians dispersed. These opportunities, therefore, gave these men their chance, and their own great qualities enabled them to profit by them, so as to ennoble their country and augment its fortunes.

Those who by the exercise of abilities such as these become princes, obtain their dominions with difficulty but retain them easily, and the difficulties which they have in acquiring their dominions arise in part from the new rules and regulations that they have to introduce in order to establish their position securely. It must be considered that there is nothing more difficult to carry out, nor more doubtful of success, nor more dangerous to handle, than to initiate a new order of things. For the reformer has enemies in all those who profit by the old order, and only lukewarm defenders in all those who would profit by the new order, this lukewarmness arising partly from fear of their adversaries, who have the laws in their favour; and partly from the incredulity of mankind, who do not truly believe in anything new until they have had actual experience of it. Thus it arises that on every opportunity for attacking the reformer, his opponents do so with the zeal of partisans, the others only defend him half-heartedly, so that between them he runs great danger. It is necessary, however, in order to investigate thoroughly this question, to examine whether these innovators are independent, or whether they depend upon others, that is to say, whether in order to carry out their designs they have to entreat or are able to compel. In the first case they invariably succeed ill, and accomplish nothing; but when they can depend on their own strength and are able to use force, they rarely fail. Thus it comes about that all armed prophets have conquered and unarmed ones failed; for besides what has been already said, the character of peoples varies, and it is easy to persuade them of a thing, but difficult to keep them in that persuasion. And so it is necessary to order things so that when they no longer believe, they can be made to believe by force. Moses, Cyrus, Theseus, and Romulus would not have been able to keep their constitutions observed for so long had they been disarmed, as happened in our own time with Fra Girolamo Savonarola, who failed entirely in his new rules when the multitude began to disbelieve in him, and he had no means of holding fast those who had believed nor of compelling the unbelievers to believe. Therefore such men as these have great difficulty in making their way, and all their dangers are met on the road and must be overcome by their own abilities; but when once they have overcome them and have begun to be held in veneration, and have suppressed those who envied them, they remain powerful and secure, honoured and happy. . . .

Chapter VII

OF NEW DOMINIONS ACQUIRED BY THE POWER OF OTHERS OR BY FORTUNE

Those who rise from private citizens to be princes merely by fortune have little trouble in rising but very much in maintaining their position. They meet with no difficulties on the way as they fly over them, but all their difficulties arise when they are established. Such are they who are granted a state either for money, or by favour of him who grants it, as happened to many in Greece, in the cities of Ionia and of the Hellespont, who were created princes by Darius in order to hold these places for his security and glory; such were also those emperors who from private citizens rose to power by bribing the army. Such as these depend absolutely on the good will and fortune of those who have raised them, both of which are extremely inconstant and unstable. . . .

With regard to these two methods of becoming a prince,—by ability or by good fortune, I will here adduce two examples which have occurred within our memory, those of Francesco Sforza and Cesare Borgia. Francesco, by appropriate means and through great abilities, from citizen became Duke of Milan, and what he had attained after a thousand difficulties he maintained with little trouble. On the other hand, Cesare Borgia, commonly called Duke Valentine, acquired the state by the influence of his father and lost it when that influence failed, and that although every measure was adopted by him and everything done that a prudent and capable man could do to establish himself firmly in a state that the arms and the favours of others had given him. For, as we have said, he who does not lay his foundations beforehand may by great abilities do so afterwards, although with great trouble to the architect and danger to the building. If, then, one considers the procedure of the duke, it will be seen how firm were the foundations he had laid to his future power, which I do not think it superfluous to examine, as I know of no better precepts for a new prince to follow than may be found in his actions; and if his measures were not successful, it was through no fault of his own but only by the most extraordinary malignity of fortune. . . .

. . . The first thing he did was to weaken the parties of the Orsini and Colonna in Rome by gaining all their adherents who were gentlemen and making them his own followers, by granting them large remuneration, and appointing them to commands and offices according to their rank, so that their attachment to their parties was extinguished in a few months, and entirely concentrated on the duke. After this he awaited an opportunity for crushing the chiefs of the Orsini, having already suppressed those of the Colonna family, and when the opportunity arrived he made good use of it. . . . He dissembled his aims so well that the Orsini made their peace with him, being represented by Signor Paulo whose suspicions the duke disarmed with every courtesy, presenting him with robes, money, and horses, so that in their simplicity they were induced to come to Sinigaglia and fell into his hands. Having thus suppressed these leaders and made their partisans his friends, the duke had laid a very good foundation to his power, having all the Romagna with the duchy of Urbino, and having gained the favour of the inhabitants, who began to feel the benefit of his rule.

And as this part is worthy of note and of imitation by others, I will not omit mention of it. When he took the Romagna, it had previously been governed by weak rulers, who had rather despoiled their subjects than governed them, and given them more cause for disunion than for union, so that the province was a prey to robbery, assaults, and every kind of disorder. He, therefore, judged it necessary to give them a good government in order to make them peaceful and obedient to his rule. For this purpose he appointed Messer Remirro de Orco, a cruel and able man, to whom he gave the fullest authority. This man, in a short time, was highly successful in rendering the country orderly and united, whereupon the duke, not deeming such excessive authority expedient, lest it should become hateful, appointed a civil court of justice in the centre of the province under an excellent president, to which each city appointed its own advocate. And as he knew that the harshness of the past had engendered some amount of hatred, in order to purge the minds of the people and to win them over completely, he resolved to show that if any cruelty had taken place it was not by his orders, but through the harsh disposition of his minister. And having found the opportunity he had him cut in half and placed one morning in the public square at Cesena with a piece of wood and bloodstained knife by his side. The ferocity of this spectacle caused the people both satisfaction and amazement. . . .

. . . But Alexander died five years after Cesare Borgia had first drawn his sword. He was left with only the state of Romagna firmly established, and all the other schemes in mid-air, between two very powerful and hostile armies, and suffering from a fatal illness. But the valour and ability of the duke were such, and he knew so well how to win over men or vanquish them, and so strong were the foundations that he had laid in this short time, that if he had not had those two armies upon him, or else had been in good health, he would have survived every difficulty. . . . And he told me on the day that Pope Julius II was elected, that he had thought of everything which might happen on the death of his father, and provided against everything, except that he had never thought that at his father's death he would be dying himself.

Reviewing thus all the actions of the duke, I find nothing to blame, on the contrary, I feel bound, as I have done, to hold him up as an example to be imitated by all who by fortune and with the arms of others have risen to power. For with his great courage and high ambition he could not have acted otherwise, and his designs were only frustrated by the short life of Alexander and his own illness. Whoever, therefore, deems it necessary in his new principality to secure himself against enemies, to gain friends, to conquer by force or fraud, to make himself beloved and feared by the people, followed and reverenced by the soldiers, to destroy those who can and may injure him, introduce innovations into old customs, to be severe and kind, magnanimous and liberal, suppress the old militia, create a new one, maintain the friendship of kings and princes in such a way that they are glad to benefit him and fear to injure him, such a one can find no better example than the actions of this man. The only thing he can be accused of is that in the creation of Julius II he made a bad choice; for, as has been said, not being able to choose his own pope, he could still prevent any one individual being made pope, and he ought never to have permitted any of those cardinals to be raised to the papacy whom he had injured, or who when pope would stand in fear of him. . . . And whoever thinks that in high personages new benefits cause old offences to be forgotten, makes a great mistake. The duke, therefore, erred in this choice, and it was the cause of his ultimate ruin.

Chapter VIII

OF THOSE WHO HAVE ATTAINED THE
POSITION OF PRINCE BY VILLAINY

But as there are still two ways of becoming prince which cannot be attributed entirely either to fortune or to ability, they must not be passed over, although one of them could be more fully discussed if we were treating of republics. These are when one becomes prince by some nefarious or villainous means, or when a private citizen becomes the prince of his country through the favour of his fellow-citizens. And in speaking of the former means, I will give two examples, one ancient, the other modern, without entering further into the merits of this method, as I judge them to be sufficient for any one obliged to imitate them.

Agathocles the Sicilian rose not only from private life but from the lowest and most abject position to be King of Syracuse. The son of a potter, he led a life of the utmost wickedness through all the stages of his fortune. Nevertheless, his wickedness was accompanied by such vigour of mind and body that, having joined the militia, he rose through its ranks to be prætor of Syracuse. Having been appointed to this position, and having decided to become prince, and to hold with violence and without the support of others that which had been constitutionally granted him; and having imparted his design to Hamilcar the Carthaginian, who was fighting with his armies in Sicily, he called together one morning the people and senate of Syracuse, as if he had to deliberate on matters of importance to the republic, and at a given signal had all the senators and the richest men of the people killed by his soldiers. After their death he occupied and held rule over the city without any civil strife. And although he was twice beaten by the Carthaginians and ultimately besieged, he was able not only to defend the city, but leaving a portion of his forces for its defence, with the remainder he invaded Africa, and in a short time liberated Syracuse from the siege and brought the Carthaginians to great extremities, so that they were obliged to come to terms with him, and remain contented with the possession of Africa, leaving Sicily to Agathocles. Whoever considers, therefore, the actions and qualities of this man, will see few if any things which can be attributed to fortune; for, as above stated, it was not by the favour of any person, but through the grades of the militia, in which he had advanced with a thousand hardships and perils, that he arrived at the position of prince, which he afterwards maintained by so many courageous and perilous expedients. It cannot be called virtue to kill one's fellow-citizens, betray one's friends, be without faith, without pity, and without religion; by these methods one may indeed gain power, but not glory. For if the virtues of Agathocles in braving and overcoming perils, and his greatness of soul in supporting and surmounting obstacles be considered, one sees no reason for holding him inferior to any of the most renowned captains. Nevertheless his barbarous cruelty and inhumanity, together with his countless atrocities, do not permit of his being named among the most famous men. We cannot attribute to fortune or virtue that which he achieved without either. . . .

Some may wonder how it came about that Agathocles, and others like him, could, after infinite treachery
and cruelty, live secure for many years in their country
and defend themselves from external enemies without
being conspired against by their subjects; although many
others have, owing to their cruelty, been unable to maintain their position in times of peace, not to speak of the
uncertain times of war. I believe this arises from the
cruelties being exploited well or badly. Well committed
may be called those (if it is permissible to use the word
well of evil) which are perpetuated once for the need of
securing one's self, and which afterwards are not per-
sisted in, but are exchanged for measures as useful to the
subjects as possible. Cruelties ill committed are those
which, although at first few, increase rather than diminish with time. Those who follow the former method
may remedy in some measure their condition, both with
God and man; as did Agathocles. As to the others, it is
impossible for them to maintain themselves.

Whence it is to be noted, that in taking a state the
conqueror must arrange to commit all his cruelties at
once, so as not to have to recur to them every day, and
so as to be able, by not making fresh changes, to reas-
sure people and win them over by benefiting them.
Whoever acts otherwise, either through timidity or bad
counsels, is always obliged to stand with knife in hand,
and can never depend on his subjects, because they,

owing to continually fresh injuries are unable to depend upon him. For injuries should be done all together, so that being less tasted, they will give less offence. Benefits should be granted little by little, so that they may be better enjoyed. And above all, a prince must live with his subjects in such a way that no accident of good or evil fortune can deflect him from his course; for necessity arising in adverse times, you are not in time with severity, and the good that you do does not profit, as it is judged to be forced upon you, and you will derive no benefit whatever from it.

Chapter IX

OF THE CIVIC PRINCIPALITY

But we now come to the case where a citizen becomes prince not through crime or intolerable violence, but by the favour of his fellow-citizens, which may be called a civic principality. To attain this position depends not entirely on worth or entirely on fortune, but rather on cunning assisted by fortune. One attains it by help of popular favour or by the favour of the aristocracy. For in every city these two opposite parties are to be found, arising from the desire of the populace to avoid the oppression of the great, and the desire of the great to command and oppress the people. And from these two opposing interests arises in the city one of the three effects: either absolute government, liberty, or licence.

The former is created either by the populace or the nobility, depending on the relative opportunities of the two parties; for when the nobility see that they are unable to resist the people they unite in exalting one of their number and creating him prince, so as to be able to carry out their own designs under the shadow of his authority. The populace, on the other hand, when unable to resist the nobility, endeavour to exalt and create a prince in order to be protected by his authority. He who becomes prince by help of the nobility has greater difficulty in maintaining his power than he who is raised by the populace, for he is surrounded by those who think themselves his equals, and is thus unable to direct or command as he pleases. But one who is raised to leadership by popular favour finds himself alone, and has no one, or very few, who are not ready to obey him. Besides which, it is impossible to satisfy the nobility by fair dealing and without inflicting injury on others, whereas it is very easy to satisfy the mass of the people in this way. For the aim of the people is more honest than that of the nobility, the latter desiring to oppress, and the former merely to avoid oppression. . . .

One, however, who becomes prince by favour of the populace, must maintain its friendship, which he will find easy, the people asking nothing but not to be oppressed. But one who against the people's wishes becomes prince by favour of the nobles, should above all endeavour to gain the favour of the people; this will be easy to him if he protects them. And as men, who receive good from whom they expected evil, feel under a greater obligation to their benefactor, so the populace will soon become even better disposed towards him than if he had become prince through their favour. The prince can win their favour in many ways, which vary according to circumstances, for which no certain rule can be given, and will therefore be passed over. I will only say, in conclusion, that it is necessary for a prince to possess the friendship of the people; otherwise he has no resource in times of adversity. . . .

Chapter X

HOW THE STRENGTH OF ALL

STATES SHOULD BE MEASURED

In examining the character of these principalities it is necessary to consider another point, namely, whether the prince has such a position as to be able in case of need to maintain himself alone, or whether he has always need of the protection of others. The better to explain this I would say, that I consider those capable of maintaining themselves alone who can, through abundance of men or money, put together a sufficient army, and hold the field against any one who assails them; and I consider to have need of others, those who cannot take the field against their enemies, but are obliged to take refuge within their walls and stand on the defensive. We have already discussed the former case and will speak of it in future as occasion arises. In the second case there is nothing to be said except to encourage such a prince to provision and fortify his own town, and not to trouble about the surrounding country. And whoever has strongly fortified his town and, as regards the government of his subjects, has proceeded as we have already described and will further relate, will be attacked with great reluctance, for men are always averse to enterprises in which they foresee difficulties, and it can never appear easy to attack one who has his town stoutly defended and is not hated by the people. . . .

Chapter XI

OF ECCLESIASTICAL PRINCIPALITIES

It now only remains to us to speak of ecclesiastical principalities, with regard to which the difficulties lie wholly before they are possessed. They are acquired either by ability or by fortune; but are maintained without either, for they are sustained by ancient religious customs, which are so powerful and of such quality, that they keep their princes in power in whatever manner they proceed and live. These princes alone have states without defending them, have subjects without governing them, and their states, not being defended, are not taken from them; their subjects not being governed do not resent it, and neither think nor are capable of alienating themselves from them. Only these principalities, therefore, are secure and happy. But as they are upheld by higher causes, which the human mind cannot attain to, I will abstain from speaking of them; for being exalted and maintained by God, it would be the work of a presumptuous and foolish man to discuss them. However, I might be asked how it has come about that the Church has reached such great temporal power, when, previous to Alexander VI, the Italian potentates—and not merely the really powerful ones, but every lord or baron, however insignificant—held it in slight esteem as regards temporal power; whereas now it is dreaded by a king of France, whom it has been able to drive out of Italy, and has also been able to ruin the Venetians. Therefore, although this is well known, I do not think it superfluous to call it to mind.

Before Charles, King of France, came into Italy, this country was under the rule of the Pope, the Venetians, the King of Naples, the Duke of Milan, and the Florentines. These potentates had to have two chief cares: one, that no foreigner should enter Italy by force of arms, the other that none of the existing governments should extend its dominions. Those chiefly to be watched were the Pope and the Venetians. To keep back the Venetians required the alliance of all the others, as in the defence of Ferrara, and to keep down the

Pope they made use of the Roman baron. These were divided into two factions, the Orsini and the Colonna, and as there was constant quarrelling between them, and they were constantly under arms, before the eye of the Pope, they kept the papacy weak and infirm. And although there arose now and then a resolute Pope like Sextus yet his fortune or ability was never able to liberate him from these evils. The shortness of their life was the reason of this, for in the course of ten years which, as a general rule, a Pope lived, he had great difficulty in suppressing even one of the factions, and if, for example, a Pope had almost put down the Colonna, a new Pope would succeed who was hostile to the Orsini, which caused the Colonna to spring up again, and he was not in time to suppress them.

This caused the temporal power of the Pope to be of little esteem in Italy. Then arose Alexander VI who, of all the pontiffs who have ever reigned, best showed how a Pope might prevail both by money and by force. With Duke Valentine as his instrument, and seizing the opportunity of the French invasion, he did all that I have previously described in speaking of the actions of the duke. And although his object was to aggrandise not the Church but the duke, what he did resulted in the aggrandizement of the Church, which after the death of the duke became the heir of his labours. Then came Pope Julius, who found the Church powerful, possessing all Romagna, all the Roman barons suppressed, and the factions destroyed by the severity of Alexander. He also found the way open for accumulating wealth in ways never used before the time of Alexander. These measures were not only followed by Julius, but increased; he resolved to gain Bologna, put down the Venetians and drive the French from Italy, in all which enterprises he was successful. He merits the greater praise, as he did everything to increase the power of the Church and not of any private person. He also kept the Orsini and Colonna parties in the condition in which he found them, and although there were some leaders among them who might have made changes, there were two things that kept them steady: one, the greatness of the Church, which they dreaded; the other, the fact that they had no cardinals, who are the origin of the tumults among them. For these parties are never at rest when they have cardinals, for these stir up the parties both within Rome and outside, and the barons are forced to defend them. Thus from the ambitions of prelates arise the discords and tumults among the barons. His holiness, Pope Leo X, therefore, has found the pontificate in a very powerful condition, from which it is hoped that as those Popes made it great by force of arms, so he through his goodness and infinite other virtues will make it both great and venerated.

Chapter XII

THE DIFFERENT KINDS OF MILITIA

AND MERCENARY SOLDIERS

Having now discussed fully the qualities of these principalities of which I proposed to treat, and partially
considered the causes of their prosperity or failure, and
having also showed the methods by which many have
sought to obtain such states, it now remains for me to
treat generally of the methods, both offensive and
defensive, that can be used in each of them. We have
said already how necessary it is for a prince to have his
foundations good, otherwise he is certain to be ruined.
The chief foundations of all states, whether new, old,
or mixed, are good laws and good arms. And as there
cannot be good laws where there are not good arms,
and where there are good arms there must be good
laws, I will not now discuss the laws, but will speak of
the arms.

I say, therefore, that the arms by which a prince
defends his possessions are either his own, or else mercenaries, or auxiliaries, or mixed. The mercenaries and
auxiliaries are useless and dangerous, and if any one sup-
ports his state by the arms of mercenaries, he will never
stand firm or sure, as they are disunited, ambitious,
without discipline, faithless, bold amongst friends, cowardly amongst enemies, they have no fear of God, and

keep no faith with men. Ruin is only deferred as long as the assault is postponed; in peace you are despoiled by them, and in war by the enemy. The cause of this is that they have no love or other motive to keep them in the field beyond a trifling wage, which is not enough to make them ready to die for you. They are quite willing to be your soldiers so long as you do not make war, but when war comes, it is either fly or decamp altogether. I ought to have little trouble in proving this, since the ruin of Italy is now caused by nothing else but through her having relied for many years on mercenary arms. These did indeed help certain individuals to power, and appeared courageous when matched against each other, but when the foreigner came they showed their worthlessness. Thus it came about that King Charles of France was allowed to take Italy without the slightest trouble, and those who said that it was owing to our sins, spoke the truth, but it was not the sins they meant but those that I have related. And as it was the sins of princes, they too have suffered the punishment. . . .

You must understand that in these latter times, as soon as the empire began to be repudiated in Italy and the Pope to gain greater reputation in temporal matters, Italy was divided into many states; many of the principal cities took up arms against their nobles, who, favoured by the emperor, had held them in subjection, and the Church encouraged this in order to increase its temporal power. In many other cities one of the inhabitants became prince. Thus Italy having fallen almost entirely into the hands of the Church and a few republics, and the priests and other citizens not being accustomed to bear arms, they began to hire foreigners as soldiers. The first to bring into reputation this kind of militia was Alberigo da Como, a native of Romagna. Braccio and Sforza, who were in their day the arbiters of Italy were, amongst others, trained by him. After these came all those others who up to the present day have commanded the armies of Italy, and the result of their prowess has been that Italy has been overrun by Charles, preyed on by Louis, tyrannized over by Ferrando, and insulted by the Swiss. The system adopted by them was, in the first place, to increase their own reputation by discrediting the infantry. They did this because, as they had no country and lived on their earnings, a few foot soldiers did not augment their reputation, and they could not maintain a large number and therefore they restricted themselves almost entirely to cavalry, by which with a smaller number they were well paid and honoured. They reduced things to such a state that in an army of 20,000 soldiers there were not 2,000 foot. They had also used every means to spare themselves and the soldiers any hardship or fear by not killing each other in their encounters, but taking prisoners without expectation of ransom. They made no attacks on fortifications by night; and those in the fortifications did not attack the tents at night, they made no stockades or ditches round their camps, and did not take the field in winter. All these things were permitted by their military code, and adopted, as we have said, to avoid trouble and danger, so that they have reduced Italy to slavery and degradation.

Chapter XIV

THE DUTIES OF A PRINCE
WITH REGARD TO THE MILITIA

A prince should therefore have no other aim or thought, nor take up any other thing for his study, but war and its organization and discipline, for that is the only art that is necessary to one who commands, and it is of such virtue that it not only maintains those who are born princes, but often enables men of private fortune to attain to that rank. And one sees, on the other hand, that when princes think more of luxury than of arms, they lose their state. The chief cause of the loss of states, is the contempt of this art, and the way to acquire them is to be well versed in the same. . . .

He ought, therefore, never to let his thoughts stray from the exercise of war; and in peace he ought to practice it more than in war, which he can do in two ways: by action and by study. As to action, he must, besides keeping his men well disciplined and exercised, engage continually in hunting, and thus accustom his body to hardships; and meanwhile learn the nature of the land, how steep the mountains are, how the valleys debouch, where the plains lie, and understand the nature of rivers and swamps. To all this he should devote great attention. This knowledge is useful in two ways. In the first place, one learns to know one's country, and can the better see how to defend it. Then by means of the knowledge and experience gained in one locality, one can easily understand any other that it may be necessary to observe; for the hills and valleys, plains and rivers of Tuscany, for instance, have a certain resemblance to those of other provinces, so that from a knowledge of the country in one province one can easily arrive at a knowledge of others. And that prince who is lacking in this skill is wanting in the first essentials of a leader; for it is this which teaches how to find the enemy, take up quarters, lead armies, plan battles and lay siege to towns with advantage. . . .

But as to exercise for the mind, the prince ought to read history and study the actions of eminent men, see how they acted in warfare, examine the causes of their victories and defeats in order to imitate the former and avoid the latter, and above all, do as some men have done in the past, who have imitated some one, who has been much praised and glorified, and have always kept his deeds and actions before them, as they say Alexander the Great imitated Achilles, Cæsar Alexander, and

Scipio Cyrus. And whoever reads the life of Cyrus written by Xenophon, will perceive in the life of Scipio how
gloriously he imitated the former, and how, in chastity,
affability, humanity, and liberality Scipio conformed to
those qualities of Cyrus as described by Xenophon. . . .

Chapter XV

OF THE THINGS FOR WHICH MEN, AND
ESPECIALLY PRINCES, ARE PRAISED OR BLAMED

It now remains to be seen what are the methods and
rules for a prince as regards his subjects and friends.
And as I know that many have written of this, I fear
that my writing about it may be deemed presumptuous,
differing as I do, especially in this matter, from the
opinions of others. But my intention being to write
something of use to those who understand, it appears to
me more proper to go to the real truth of the matter
than to its imagination; and many have imagined republics and principalities which have never been seen or
known to exist in reality; for how we live is so far
removed from how we ought to live, that he who aban-
dons what is done for what ought to be done, will rather
learn to bring about his own ruin than his preservation.
A man who wishes to make a profession of goodness in
everything must necessarily come to grief among so
many who are not good. Therefore it is necessary for a
prince, who wishes to maintain himself, to learn how

not to be good, and to use this knowledge and not use it, according to the necessity of the case.

Leaving on one side, then, those things which concern only an imaginary prince, and speaking of those that are real, I state that all men, and especially princes, who are placed at a greater height, are reputed for certain qualities which bring them either praise or blame. Thus one is considered liberal, another *misero* or miserly (using a Tuscan term, seeing that *avaro* with us still means one who is rapaciously acquisitive and *misero* one who makes grudging use of his own); one a free giver, another rapacious; one cruel, another merciful; one a breaker of his word, another trustworthy; one effeminate and pusillanimous, another fierce and high-spirited; one humane, another haughty; one lascivious, another chaste; one frank, another astute; one hard, another easy; one serious, another frivolous; one religious, another an unbeliever, and so on. I know that every one will admit that it would be highly praiseworthy in a prince to possess all the above-named qualities that are reputed good, but as they cannot all be possessed or observed, human conditions not permitting of it, it is necessary that he should be prudent enough to avoid the scandal of those vices which would lose him the state, and guard himself if possible against those which will not lose it him, but if not able to, he can indulge them with less scruple. And yet he must not mind incurring the scandal of those vices, without which it would be difficult to save the state, for if one considers well, it will be found that some things which seem virtues would, if followed, lead to one's ruin, and some others which appear vices result in one's greater security and wellbeing.

Chapter XVI
OF LIBERALITY AND NIGGARDLINESS

Beginning now with the first qualities above named, I say that it would be well to be considered liberal; nevertheless liberality such as the world understands it will injure you, because if used virtuously and in the proper way, it will not be known, and you will incur the disgrace of the contrary vice. But one who wishes to obtain the reputation of liberality among men, must not omit every kind of sumptuous display, and to such an extent that a prince of this character will consume by such means all his resources, and will be at last compelled, if he wishes to maintain his name for liberality, to impose heavy taxes on his people, become extortionate, and do everything possible to obtain money. This will make his subjects begin to hate him, and he will be little esteemed being poor, so that having by this liberality injured many and benefited but few, he will feel the first little disturbance and be endangered by every peril. If he recognises this and wishes to change his system, he incurs at once the charge of niggardliness.

. . . In course of time he will be thought more liberal, when it is seen that by his parsimony his revenue is sufficient, that he can defend himself against those who make war on him, and undertake enterprises without burdening his people, so that he is really liberal to all those from whom he does not take, who are infinite in number, and niggardly to all to whom he does not give, who are few. In our times we have seen nothing great done except by those who have been esteemed niggardly; the others have all been ruined. Pope Julius II, although he had made use of a reputation for liberality in order to attain the papacy, did not seek to retain it afterwards, so that he might be able to wage war. The present King of France has carried on so many wars without imposing an extraordinary tax, because his extra expenses were covered by the parsimony he had so long practiced. The present King of Spain, if he had been thought liberal, would not have engaged in and been successful in so many enterprises. . . .

. . . And you may be very generous indeed with what is not the property of yourself or your subjects, as were Cyrus, Cæsar, and Alexander; for spending the wealth of others will not diminish your reputation, but increase it, only spending your own resources will injure you. There is nothing which destroys itself so much as liberality, for by using it you lose the power of using it, and become either poor and despicable, or, to escape poverty, rapacious and hated. And of all things that a prince must guard against, the most important are being despicable or hated, and liberality will lead you to one or other of these conditions. . . .

Chapter XVII

OF CRUELTY AND CLEMENCY, AND WHETHER
IT IS BETTER TO BE LOVED OR FEARED

Proceeding to the other qualities before named, I say that every prince must desire to be considered merciful and not cruel. He must, however, take care not to misuse this mercifulness. Cesare Borgia was considered cruel, but his cruelty had brought order to the Romagna, united it, and reduced it to peace and fealty. If this is considered well, it will be seen that he was really much more merciful than the Florentine people, who, to avoid the name of cruelty, allowed Pistoia to be destroyed. A prince, therefore, must not mind incurring the charge of cruelty for the purpose of keeping his subjects united and faithful; for, with a very few examples, he will be more merciful than those who, from excess of tenderness, allow disorders to arise, from whence spring bloodshed and rapine; for these as a rule injure the whole community, while the executions carried out by the prince injure only individuals. And of all princes, it is impossible for a new prince to escape the reputation of cruelty, new states being always full of dangers. . . .

From this arises the question whether it is better to be loved more than feared, or feared more than loved. The reply is, that one ought to be both feared and loved, but as it is difficult for the two to go together, it is much safer to be feared than loved, if one of the two has to be wanting. For it may be said of men in general that they are ungrateful, voluble, dissemblers, anxious to avoid danger, and covetous of gain; as long as you benefit them, they are entirely yours; they offer you their blood, their goods, their life, and their children, as I have before said, when the necessity is remote; but when it approaches, they revolt. And the prince who has relied solely on their words, without making other preparations, is ruined; for the friendship which is gained by purchase and not through grandeur and nobility of spirit is bought but not secured, and at a pinch is not to be expended in your service. And men have less scruple in offending one who makes himself loved than one who makes himself feared; for love is held by a chain of obligation which, men being selfish, is broken whenever it serves their purpose; but fear is maintained by a dread of punishment which never fails.

Still, a prince should make himself feared in such a way that if he does not gain love, he at any rate avoids hatred: for fear and the absence of hatred may well go together, and will be always attained by one who abstains from interfering with the property of his citizens and subjects or with their women. And when he is obliged to take the life of any one, let him do so when there is a proper justification and manifest reason for it; but above all he must abstain from taking the property of others, for men forget more easily the death of their father than the loss of their patrimony. . . .

But when the prince is with his army and has a large number of soldiers under his control, then it is extremely necessary that he should not mind being thought cruel; for without this reputation he could not keep an army united or disposed to any duty. Among the noteworthy actions of Hannibal is numbered this, that although he had an enormous army, composed of men of all nations and fighting in foreign countries, there never arose any dissension either among them or against the prince, either in good fortune or in bad. This could not be due to anything but his inhuman cruelty, which together with his infinite other virtues, made him always venerated and terrible in the sight of his soldiers, and without it his other virtues would not have sufficed to produce that effect. Thoughtless writers admire on the one hand his actions, and on the other blame the principal cause of them. . . .

Chapter XVIII

IN WHAT WAY PRINCES MUST KEEP FAITH

How laudable it is for a prince to keep good faith and live with integrity, and not with astuteness, every one knows. Still the experience of our times shows those princes to have done great things who have had little regard for good faith, and have been able by astuteness to confuse men's brains, and who have ultimately overcome those who have made loyalty their foundation.

You must know, then, that there are two methods of fighting, the one by law, the other by force: the first method is that of men, the second of beasts; but as the first method is often insufficient, one must have recourse to the second. It is therefore necessary for a prince to know well how to use both the beast and the man. This was covertly taught to rulers by ancient writers, who relate how Achilles and many others of those ancient princes were given to Chiron the centaur to be brought up and educated under his discipline. The parable of this semi-animal, semi-human teacher is meant to indicate that a prince must know how to use both natures, and that the one without the other is not durable.

A prince being thus obliged to know well how to act as a beast must imitate the fox and the lion, for the lion cannot protect himself from traps, and the fox cannot defend himself from wolves. One must therefore be a fox to recognise traps, and a lion to frighten wolves. Those that wish to be only lions do not understand this. Therefore, a prudent ruler ought not to keep faith when by so doing it would be against his interest, and when the reasons which made him bind himself no longer exist. If men were all good, this precept would not be a good one; but as they are bad, and would not observe their faith with you, so you are not bound to keep faith with them. Nor have legitimate grounds ever failed a prince who wished to show colourable excuse for the non-fulfilment of his promise. Of this one could furnish an infinite number of modern examples, and show how many times peace has been broken, and how many promises rendered worthless, by the faithlessness of princes, and those that have been best able to imitate the fox have succeeded best. But it is necessary to be able to disguise this character well, and to be a great feigner and dissembler; and men are so simple and so ready to obey present necessities, that one who deceives will always find those who allow themselves to be deceived.

I will only mention one modern instance. Alexander VI did nothing else but deceive men, he thought of nothing else, and found the occasion for it; no man was ever more able to give assurances, or affirmed things with stronger oaths, and no man observed them less; however, he always succeeded in his deceptions, as he well knew this aspect of things.

It is not, therefore, necessary for a prince to have all the above-named qualities, but it is very necessary to seem to have them. I would even be bold to say that to possess them and always to observe them is dangerous, but to appear to possess them is useful. Thus it is well to seem merciful, faithful, humane, sincere, religious, and also to be so; but you must have the mind so disposed that when it is needful to be otherwise you may be able to change to the opposite qualities. And it must be understood that a prince, and especially a new prince, cannot observe all those things which are considered good in men, being often obliged, in order to maintain the state, to act against faith, against charity, against humanity, and against religion. And, therefore, he must have a mind disposed to adapt itself according to the wind, and as the variations of fortune dictate, and, as I said before, not deviate from what is good, if possible, but be able to do evil if constrained. . . .

Chapter XIX

THAT WE MUST AVOID BEING DESPISED AND HATED

But as I have now spoken of the most important of the qualities in question, I will now deal briefly and generally with the rest. The prince must, as already stated, avoid those things which will make him hated or despised; and whenever he succeeds in this, he will have done his part, and will find no danger in other vices. He will chiefly become hated, as I said, by being rapacious, and usurping the property and women of his subjects, which he must abstain from doing, and whenever one does not attack the property or honour of the generality of men, they will live contented; and one will only have to combat the ambition of a few, who can be easily held in check in many ways. He is rendered despicable by being thought changeable, frivolous, effeminate, timid, and irresolute; which a prince must guard against as a rock of danger, and so contrive that his actions show grandeur, spirit, gravity, and fortitude; and as to the government of his subjects, let his sentence be irrevocable, and let him adhere to his decisions so that no one may think of deceiving or cozening him. . . .

Among the kingdoms that are well ordered and governed in our time is France, and there we find numberless good institutions on which depend the liberty and security of the king; of these the chief is the parliament and its authority, because he who established that kingdom, knowing the ambition and insolence of the great nobles, deemed it necessary to have a bit in their mouths to check them. And knowing on the other hand the hatred of the mass of the people against the great, based on fear, and wishing to secure them, he did not wish to make this the special care of the king, to relieve him of the dissatisfaction that he might incur among the nobles by favouring the people, and among the people by favouring the nobles. He therefore established a third judge that, without direct charge of the king, kept in check the great and favoured the lesser people. Nor could any better or more prudent measure have been adopted, nor better precaution for the safety of the king and the kingdom. From which another notable rule can be drawn, that princes should let the carrying out of unpopular duties devolve on others, and bestow favours themselves. I conclude again by saying that a prince must esteem his nobles, but not make himself hated by the populace. . . .

Considering, on the other hand, the qualities of Commodus, Severus, Antoninus, Caracalla, and Maximinus, you will find them extremely cruel and rapacious; to satisfy the soldiers there was no injury which they would not inflict on the people, and all except Severus ended badly. . . .

Whoever examines in detail the actions of Severus, will find him to have been a very ferocious lion and an extremely astute fox, and will find him to have been feared and respected by all and not hated by the army; and will not be surprised that he, a new man, should have been able to hold so much power, since his great reputation defended him always from the hatred that his rapacity might have produced in the people. But Antoninus his son was also a man of great ability, and possessed qualities that rendered him admirable in the sight of the people and also made him popular with the soldiers, for he was a military man, capable of enduring the most extreme hardships, disdainful of delicate food, and every other luxury, which made him loved by all the armies. However, his ferocity and cruelty were so great and unheard of, through his having, after executing many private individuals, caused a large part of the population of Rome and all that of Alexandria to be killed, that he became hated by all the world and began to be feared by those about him to such an extent that he was finally killed by a centurion in the midst of his army. . . .

Chapter XX

WHETHER FORTRESSES AND OTHER THINGS WHICH PRINCES OFTEN CONTRIVE ARE USEFUL OR INJURIOUS

Some princes, in order to hold their possessions securely, have disarmed their citizens, some others have kept their subject lands divided into parts, others have fomented enmities against themselves, others have endeavoured to win over those whom they suspected at the commencement of their rule: some have constructed fortresses, others have cast them down and destroyed them. And although one cannot pronounce a definite judgment as to these things without going into the particulars of the state to which such a deliberation is to be applied, still I will speak in such a general way as the matter will permit. . . .

Our forefathers and those who were esteemed wise used to say that it was necessary to hold Pistoia by means of factions and Pisa with fortresses, and for this purpose they fomented differences in some of their subject towns in order to possess them more easily. In those days when there was a balance of power in Italy, this was doubtless well done, but does not seem to me to be a good precept for the present time, for I do not believe that the divisions thus created ever do any good; on the contrary it is certain that when the enemy approaches, the cities thus divided will be at once lost, for the weaker faction will always side with the enemy and the other will not be able to stand. . . .

It has been the custom of princes in order to be able to hold their state securely, to erect fortresses, as a bridle and bit to those who have designs against them, and in order to have a secure refuge against a sudden assault. I approve this method, because it was anciently used. Nevertheless, Messer Niccolò Vitelli has been seen in our own time to destroy two fortresses in Città di Castello in order to keep that state. Guid'Ubaldo, Duke of Urbino, on returning to his dominions from which he had been driven by Cesare Borgia, razed to their foundations all the fortresses of that province, and considered that without them it would be more difficult for him to lose the state again. The Bentivogli, in returning to Bologna, took similar measures. Therefore fortresses may or may not be useful according to the times; if they do good in one way, they do harm in another. The question may be discussed thus: a prince who fears his own people more than foreigners ought to build fortresses, but he who has greater fear of foreigners than of his own people ought to do without them. The castle of Milan built by Francesco Sforza has given and will give more trouble to the house of Sforza than any other disorder in that state. Therefore the best fortress is to be found in the love of the people, for although you may have fortresses they will not save you if you are hated by the people. When once the people have taken arms against you, there will never be lacking foreigners to assist them. In our times we do not see that they have profited any ruler, except the Countess of Forlì on the death of her consort Count Girolamo, for she was thus enabled to escape the popular rising and await help from Milan and recover the state; the circumstances being then such that no foreigner could assist the people. But afterwards they were of little use to her when Cesare Borgia attacked her and the people being hostile to her allied themselves with the foreigner. So that then and before it would have been safer for her not to have been hated by the people than to have had the fortresses. Having considered these things I would therefore praise the one who erects fortresses and the one who does not, and would blame any one who, trusting in them, recks little of being hated by his people.

Chapter XXI

HOW A PRINCE MUST ACT IN
ORDER TO GAIN REPUTATION

Nothing causes a prince to be so much esteemed as great enterprises and giving proof of prowess. We have in our own day Ferdinand, King of Aragon, the present King of Spain. He may almost be termed a new prince, because from a weak king he has become for fame and glory the first king in Christendom, and if you regard his actions you will find them all very great and some of them extraordinary. At the beginning of his reign he assailed Granada, and that enterprise was the foundation of his state. At first he did it at his leisure and without fear of being interfered with; he kept the minds of the barons of Castile occupied in this enterprise, so that thinking only of that war they did not think of making innovations, and he thus acquired reputation and power over them without their being aware of it. He was able with the money of the Church and the people to maintain his armies, and by that long war to lay the foundations of his military power, which afterwards has made him famous. Besides this, to be able to undertake greater enterprises, and always under the pretext of religion, he had recourse to a pious cruelty, driving out the Moors from his kingdom and despoiling them. No more miserable or unusual example can be found. He also attacked Africa under the same pretext, undertook his Italian enterprise, and has lately attacked France; so that he has continually contrived great things, which have kept his subjects' minds uncertain and astonished, and occupied in watching their result. And these actions have arisen one out of the other, so that they have left no time for men to settle down and act against him. . . .

A prince must also show himself a lover of merit, give preferment to the able, and honour those who excel in every art. Moreover he must encourage his citizens to follow their callings quietly, whether in commerce, or agriculture, or any other trade that men follow, so that this one shall not refrain from improving his possessions through fear that they may be taken from him, and that one from starting a trade for fear of taxes; but he should offer rewards to whoever does these things, and to whoever seeks in any way to improve his city or state. Besides this, he ought, at convenient seasons of the year, to keep the people occupied with festivals and shows; and as every city is divided either into guilds or into classes, he ought to pay attention to all these groups, mingle with them from time to time and give them an example of his humanity and munificence, always upholding, however, the majesty of his dignity, which must never be allowed to fail in anything whatever.

Chapter XXIII

HOW FLATTERERS MUST BE SHUNNED

I must not omit an important subject, and mention of a mistake which princes can with difficulty avoid, if they are not very prudent, or if they do not make a good choice. And this is with regard to flatterers, of which courts are full, because men take such pleasure in their own things and deceive themselves about them that they can with difficulty guard against this plague; and by wishing to guard against it they run the risk of becoming contemptible. Because there is no other way of guarding one's self against flattery than by letting men understand that they will not offend you by speaking the truth; but when every one can tell you the truth, you lose their respect. A prudent prince must therefore take a third course, by choosing for his council wise men, and giving these alone full liberty to speak the truth to him, but only of those things that he asks and of nothing else; but he must ask them about everything and hear their opinion, and afterwards deliberate by himself in his own way, and in these councils and with each of these men comport himself so that every one may see that the more freely he speaks, the more he will be acceptable. Beyond these he should listen to no one, go about the matter deliberately, and be determined in his decisions. Whoever acts otherwise either acts precipitately through flattery or else changes often through the variety of opinions, from which it follows that he will be little esteemed. . . .

A prince, therefore, ought always to take counsel, but only when he wishes, not when others wish; on the contrary he ought to discourage absolutely attempts to advise him unless he asks it, but he ought to be a great asker, and a patient hearer of the truth about those things of which he has inquired; indeed, if he finds that any one has scruples in telling him the truth he should

be angry. And since some think that a prince who gains
the reputation of being prudent is so considered, not by
his nature but by the good counsellors he has about
him, they are undoubtedly deceived. It is an infallible
rule that a prince who is not wise himself cannot be
well advised, unless by chance he leaves himself entirely
in the hands of one man who rules him in everything,
and happens to be a very prudent man. In this case he
may doubtless be well governed, but it would not last
long, for that governor would in a short time deprive
him of the state; but by taking counsel with many, a
prince who is not wise will never have united councils
and will not be able to bring them to unanimity for
himself. The counsellors will all think of their own
interests, and he will be unable either to correct or to
understand them. And it cannot be otherwise, for men
will always be false to you unless they are compelled by
necessity to be true. Therefore it must be concluded
that wise counsels, from whoever they come, must necessarily be due to the prudence of the prince, and not
the prudence of the prince to the good counsels received.

Chapter XXIV

WHY THE PRINCES OF ITALY HAVE LOST THEIR STATES

The before-mentioned things, if prudently observed,
make a new prince seem ancient, and render him at once
more secure and firmer in the state than if he had been

established there of old. For a new prince is much more observed in his actions than a hereditary one, and when these are recognised as virtuous, he wins over men more and they are more bound to him than if he were of the ancient blood. For men are much more taken by present than by past things, and when they find themselves well off in the present, they enjoy it and seek nothing more; on the contrary, they will do all they can to defend him, so long as the prince is not in other things deficient. And thus he will have the double glory of having founded a new realm and adorned it and fortified it with good laws, good arms, good friends and good examples; as he will have double shame who is born a prince and through want of prudence has lost his throne.

And if one considers those rulers who have lost their position in Italy in our days, such as the King of Naples, the Duke of Milan and others, one will find in them first a common defect as to their arms, for the reasons discussed at length, then we observe that some of them either had the people hostile to them, or that if the people were friendly they were not able to make sure of the nobility, for without these defects, states are not lost that have enough strength to be able to keep an army in the field. Philip of Macedon, not the father of Alexander the Great, but the one who was conquered by Titus Quintius, did not possess a great state compared to the greatness of Rome and Greece which assailed him, but being a military man and one who knew how to ingratiate himself with the people and make sure of the great, he was able to sustain the war against them for many years; and if at length he lost his power over some cities, he was still able to keep his kingdom.

Therefore, those of our princes who had held their possessions for many years must not accuse fortune for having lost them, but rather their own remissness; for having never in quiet times considered that things might change (as it is a common fault of men not to reckon on storms in fair weather) when adverse times came, they only thought of fleeing, instead of defending themselves; and hoped that the people, enraged by the insolence of the conquerors, would recall them. This measure, when others are wanting, is good; but it is very bad to have neglected the other remedies for that one, for nobody would desire to fall because he believed that he would then find some one to pick him up. This may or may not take place, and if it does, it does not afford you security, as you have not helped yourself but been helped like a coward. Only those defences are good, certain and durable, which depend on yourself alone and your own ability.

Chapter XXV

HOW MUCH FORTUNE CAN DO IN HUMAN

AFFAIRS AND HOW IT MAY BE OPPOSED

It is not unknown to me how many have been and are of opinion that worldly events are so governed by fortune and by God, that men cannot by their prudence change them, and that on the contrary there is no remedy whatever, and for this they may judge it to be useless to toil much about them, but let things be ruled by chance. This opinion has been more held in our day, from the great changes that have been seen, and are daily seen, beyond every human conjecture. When I think about them, at times I am partly inclined to share this opinion. Nevertheless, that our free-will may not be altogether extinguished, I think it may be true that fortune is the ruler of half our actions, but that she allows the other half or thereabouts to be governed by us. I would compare her to an impetuous river that, when turbulent, inundates the plains, casts down trees and buildings, removes earth from this side and places it on the other; every one flees before it, and everything yields to its fury without being able to oppose it; and yet though it is of such a kind, still when it is quiet, men can make provision against it by dykes and banks, so that when it rises it will either go into a canal or its rush will not be so wild and dangerous. So it is with fortune, which shows her power where no measures have been taken to resist her, and directs her fury where she knows that no dykes or barriers have been made to hold her. And if you regard Italy, which has been the seat of these changes, and who has given the impulse to them, you will see her to be a country without dykes or banks of any kind. If she had been protected by proper measures, like Germany, Spain, and France, this inundation would not have caused the great changes that it has, or would not have happened at all.

This must suffice as regards opposition to fortune in general. But limiting myself more to particular cases, I would point out how one sees a certain prince to-day fortunate and to-morrow ruined, without seeing that he has changed in character or otherwise. I believe this arises in the first place from the causes that we have already discussed at length; that is to say, because the prince who bases himself entirely on fortune is ruined when fortune changes. I also believe that he is happy whose mode of procedure accords with the needs of the times, and similarly he is unfortunate whose mode of procedure is opposed to the times. For one sees that men in those things which lead them to the aim that each one has in view, namely, glory and riches, proceed in various ways; one with circumspection, another with impetuosity, one by violence, another by cunning, one with patience, another with the reverse; and each by these diverse ways may arrive at his aim. One sees also two cautious men, one of whom succeeds in his designs, and the other not, and in the same way two men succeed equally by different methods, one being cautious, the other impetuous, which arises only from the nature of the times, which does or does not conform to their method of procedure. From this it results, as I have said, that two men, acting differently, attain the same effect, and of two others acting in the same way, one attains his goal and not the other. On this depend also the changes in prosperity, for if it happens that time and circumstances are favourable to one who acts with caution and prudence he will be successful, but if time and circumstances change he will be ruined, because he does not change his mode of procedure. No man is found so prudent as to be able to adapt himself to this, either because he cannot deviate from that to which his nature disposes him, or else because having always prospered by walking in one path, he cannot persuade himself that it is well to leave it; and therefore the cautious man, when it is time to act suddenly, does not know how to do so and is consequently ruined; for if one could change one's nature with time and circumstances, fortune would never change.

Pope Julius II acted impetuously in everything he did and found the times and conditions so in conformity with that mode of procedure, that he always obtained a good result. Consider the first war that he made against Bologna while Messer Giovanni Bentivogli was still living. The Venetians were not pleased with it, neither was the King of Spain, France was conferring with him over the enterprise, notwithstanding which, owing to his fierce and impetuous disposition, he engaged personally in the expedition. This move caused both Spain and the Venetians to halt and hesitate, the latter through fear, the former through the desire to recover the entire kingdom of Naples. On the other hand, he engaged with him the King of France, because seeing him make this move and desiring his friendship in order to put down the Venetians, that king judged that he could not refuse him his troops without manifest injury. Thus Julius by his impetuous move achieved what no other pontiff with the utmost human prudence would have succeeded in doing, because, if he had waited till all arrangements had been made and everything settled before leaving Rome, as any other pontiff would have done, it would never have succeeded. For the king of France would have found a thousand excuses, and the others would have inspired him with a thousand fears. I will omit his other actions, which were all of this kind and which all succeeded well, and the shortness of his life did not suffer him to experience the contrary, for had times followed in which it was necessary to act with caution, his ruin would have resulted, for he would never have deviated from these methods to which his nature disposed him.

I conclude then that fortune varying and men remaining fixed in their ways, they are successful so long as these ways conform to circumstances, but when they are opposed then they are unsuccessful. I certainly think that it is better to be impetuous than cautious, for fortune is a woman, and it is necessary, if you wish to master her, to conquer her by force; and it can be seen that she lets herself be overcome by the bold rather than by those who proceed coldly. And therefore, like a woman, she is always a friend to the young, because they are less cautious, fiercer, and master her with greater audacity.

Chapter XXVI

EXHORTATION TO LIBERATE ITALY

FROM THE BARBARIANS

Having now considered all the things we have spoken of, and thought within myself whether at present the time was not propitious in Italy for a new prince, and if there was not a state of things which offered an opportunity to a prudent and capable man to introduce a new system that would do honour to himself and good to the mass of the people, it seems to me that so many things concur to favour a new ruler that I do not know of any time more fitting for such an enterprise. And if, as I said, it was necessary in order that the power of Moses should be displayed that the people of Israel should be slaves in Egypt, and to give scope for the greatness and courage of Cyrus that the Persians should be oppressed by the Medes, and to illustrate the preeminence of Theseus that the Athenians should be dispersed, so at the present time, in order that the might of an Italian genius might be recognised, it was necessary that Italy should be reduced to her present condition, and that she should be more enslaved than the Hebrews, more oppressed than the Persians, and more scattered than the Athenians; without a head, without order, beaten, despoiled, lacerated, and overrun, and that she should have suffered ruin of every kind.

And although before now a gleam of hope has appeared which gave hope that some individual might be appointed by God for her redemption, yet at the highest summit of his career he was thrown aside by fortune, so that now, almost lifeless, she awaits one who may heal her wounds and put a stop to the pillaging of Lombardy, to the rapacity and extortion in the Kingdom of Naples and in Tuscany, and cure her of those sores which have long been festering. Behold how she prays God to send some one to redeem her from this barbarous cruelty and insolence. Behold her ready and willing to follow any standard if only there be some one to raise it. There is nothing now she can hope for but that your illustrious house may place itself at the head of this redemption, being by its power and fortune so exalted, and being favoured by God and the Church, of which it is now the ruler. Nor will this be very difficult, if you call to mind the actions and lives of the men I have named. And although those men were rare and marvellous, they were none the less men, and each of them had less opportunity than the present, for their enterprise was not juster than this, nor easier, nor was God more their friend than He is yours. . . .

If your illustrious house, therefore, wishes to follow

those great men who redeemed their countries, it is before all things necessary, as the true foundation of every undertaking, to provide yourself with your own forces, for you cannot have more faithful, or truer and better soldiers. And although each one of them may be good, they will united become even better when they see themselves commanded by their prince, and honoured and favoured by him. It is therefore necessary to prepare such forces in order to be able with Italian prowess to defend the country from foreigners. And although both the Swiss and Spanish infantry are deemed terrible, none the less they each have their defects, so that a third method of array might not only oppose them, but be confident of overcoming them. For the Spaniards cannot sustain the attack of cavalry, and the Swiss have to fear infantry which meets them with resolution equal to their own. From which it has resulted, as will be seen by experience, that the Spaniards cannot sustain the attack of French cavalry, and the Swiss are overthrown by Spanish infantry. And although a complete example of the latter has not been seen, yet an instance was furnished in the battle of Ravenna, where the Spanish infantry attacked the German battalions, which are organised in the same way as the Swiss. The Spaniards, through their bodily agility and aided by their bucklers, had entered between and under their pikes and were in a position to attack them safely without the Germans being able to defend themselves; and if the cavalry had not charged them they would have utterly destroyed them. Knowing therefore the defects of both these kinds of infantry, a third kind can be created which can resist cavalry and need not fear infantry, and this will be done by the choice of arms and a new organisation. And these are the things which, when newly introduced, give reputation and grandeur to a new prince.

This opportunity must not, therefore, be allowed to pass, so that Italy may at length find her liberator. I cannot express the love with which he would be received in all those provinces which have suffered under these foreign invasions, with what thirst for vengeance, with what steadfast faith, with what love, with what grateful tears. What doors would be closed against him? What people would refuse him obedience? What envy could oppose him? What Italian would withhold allegiance? This barbarous domination stinks in the nostrils of every one. May your illustrious house therefore assume this task with that courage and those hopes which are inspired by a just cause, so that under its banner our fatherland may be raised up, and under its auspices be verified that saying of Petrarch:

Valour against fell wrath
Will take up arms; and be the combat quickly sped!
For, sure, the ancient worth,
That in Italians stirs the heart, is not yet dead.

DISCOURSES
ON THE
FIRST TEN BOOKS OF TITUS LIVIUS.
Translated from the Italian by Christian E. Detmold

NICCOLÒ MACHIAVELLI
TO
ZANOBI BUONDELMONTE AND
COSIMO RUCELLAI,
GREETING

With this I send you a gift which, if it bears no proportion to the extent of the obligations which I owe you, is nevertheless the best that I am able to offer to you; for I have endeavored to embody in it all that long experience and assiduous research have taught me of the affairs of the world. And as neither yourselves nor any one else can ask more than that of me, you cannot complain of my lack of talent when my arguments are poor, and of the fallacies of my judgment on account of the errors into which I have doubtless fallen many times. This being so, however, I know not which of us has the greater right to complain,—I, that you should have forced me to write what I should never have attempted of my own accord, or you, that I should have written without giving you cause to be satisfied.

Accept it, then, as one accepts whatever comes from friends, looking rather to the intention of him who gives, than to the thing offered. And believe me, that I feel a satisfaction in this, that, even if I have often erred in the course of this work, I have assuredly made no mistake in having chosen you above all other friends to whom to dedicate these discourses. In doing this, I give some proof of gratitude, although I may seem to have departed from the ordinary usage of writers, who generally dedicate their works to some prince; and, blinded by ambition or avarice, praise him for all the virtuous qualities he has not, instead of censuring him for his real vices, whilst I, to avoid this fault, do not address myself to such as are princes, but to those who by their infinite good qualities are worthy to be such; not to those who could load me with honors, rank, and wealth, but rather to those who have the desire to do so, but have not the power. For to judge rightly, men should esteem rather those who are, and not those who can be generous; and those who would know how to govern states, rather than those who have the right to govern, but lack the knowledge.

For this reason have historians praised Hiero of Syracuse, a mere private citizen, more than Perseus of Macedon, monarch though he was; for Hiero only lacked a principality to be a prince, whilst the other had nothing of the king except the diadem. Be it good or bad, however, you wanted this work, and such as it is I send it to you; and should you continue in the belief that my opinions are acceptable to you, I shall not fail to continue to examine this history, as I promised you in the beginning of it. Farewell!

FIRST BOOK

Introduction

Although the envious nature of men, so prompt to blame and so slow to praise, makes the discovery and introduction of any new principles and systems as dangerous almost as the exploration of unknown seas and continents, yet, animated by that desire which impels me to do what may prove for the common benefit of all, I have resolved to open a new route, which has not yet been followed by any one, and may prove difficult and troublesome, but may also bring me some reward in the approbation of those who will kindly appreciate my efforts.

And if my poor talents, my little experience of the present and insufficient study of the past, should make the result of my labors defective and of little utility, I shall at least have shown the way to others, who will carry out my views with greater ability, eloquence, and judgment, so that if I do not merit praise, I ought at least not to incur censure.

When we consider the general respect for antiquity,

and how often—to say nothing of other examples—a great price is paid for some fragments of an antique statue, which we are anxious to possess to ornament our houses with, or to give to artists who strive to imitate them in their own works; and when we see, on the other hand, the wonderful examples which the history of ancient kingdoms and republics presents to us, the prodigies of virtue and of wisdom displayed by the kings, captains, citizens, and legislators who have sacrificed themselves for their country,—when we see these, I say, more admired than imitated, or so much neglected that not the least trace of this ancient virtue remains, we cannot but be at the same time as much surprised as afflicted. The more so as in the differences which arise between citizens, or in the maladies to which they are subjected, we see these same people have recourse to the judgments and the remedies prescribed by the ancients. The civil laws are in fact nothing but decisions given by their jurisconsults, and which, reduced to a system, direct our modern jurists in their decisions. And what is the science of medicine, but the experience of ancient physicians, which their successors have taken for their guide? And yet to found a republic, maintain states, to govern a kingdom, organize an army, conduct a war, dispense justice, and extend empires, you will find neither prince, nor republic, nor captain, nor citizen, who has recourse to the examples of antiquity! This neglect, I am persuaded, is due less to the weakness to which the vices of our education have reduced the world, than to the evils caused by the proud indolence which prevails in most of the Christian states, and to the lack of real knowledge of history, the true sense of which is not known, or the spirit of which they do not comprehend. Thus the majority of those who read it take pleasure only in the variety of the events which history relates, without ever thinking of imitating the noble actions, deeming that not only difficult, but impossible; as though heaven, the sun, the elements, and men had changed the order of their motions and power, and were different from what they were in ancient times.

Wishing, therefore, so far as in me lies, to draw mankind from this error, I have thought it proper to write upon those books of Titus Livius that have come to us entire despite the malice of time; touching upon all those matters which, after a comparison between the ancient and modern events, may seem to me necessary to facilitate their proper understanding. In this way those who read my remarks may derive those advantages which should be the aim of all study of history; and although the undertaking is difficult, yet, aided by those who have encouraged me in this attempt, I hope to carry it sufficiently far, so that but little may remain for others to carry it to its destined end.

Chapter I

OF THE BEGINNING OF CITIES IN GENERAL,

AND ESPECIALLY THAT OF THE CITY OF ROME

Those who read what the beginning of Rome was, and what her lawgivers and her organization, will not be astonished that so much virtue should have maintained itself during so many centuries; and that so great an empire should have sprung from it afterwards. To speak first of her origin, we will premise that all cities are founded either by natives of the country or by strangers. The little security which the natives found in living dispersed; the impossibility for each to resist isolated, either because of the situation or because of their small number, the attacks of any enemy that might present himself; the difficulty of uniting in time for defence at his approach, and the necessity of abandoning the greater number of their retreats, which quickly became a prize to the assailant,—such were the motives that caused the first inhabitants of a country to build cities for the purpose of escaping these dangers. They resolved, of their own accord, or by the advice of some one who had most authority amongst them, to live together in some place of their selection that might offer them greater conveniences and greater facility of defence. Thus, amongst many others were Athens and Venice; the first was built under the authority of

Theseus, who had gathered the dispersed inhabitants; and the second owed its origin to the fact that several tribes had taken refuge on the little islands situated at the head of the Adriatic Sea, to escape from war, and from the Barbarians who after the fall of the Roman Empire had overrun Italy. These refugees of themselves, and without any prince to govern them, began to live under such laws as seemed to them best suited to maintain their new state. In this they succeeded, happily favored by the long peace, for which they were indebted to their situation upon a sea without issue, where the people that ravaged Italy could not harass them, being without any ships. Thus from that small beginning they attained that degree of power in which we see them now.

The second case is when a city is built by strangers; these may be either freemen, or subjects of a republic or of a prince, who, to relieve their states from an excessive population, or to defend a newly acquired territory which they wish to preserve without expense, send colonies there. The Romans founded many cities in this way within their empire. Sometimes cities are built by a prince, not for the purpose of living there, but merely as monuments to his glory; such was Alexandria, built by Alexander the Great. But as all these cities are at their very origin deprived of liberty, they rarely succeed in making great progress, or in being counted amongst the great powers. Such was the origin of Florence; for it was built either by the soldiers of Sylla, or perhaps by the inhabitants of Mount Fiesole, who, trusting to the long peace that prevailed in the reign of Octavian, were attracted to the plains along the Arno. Florence, thus built under the Roman Empire, could in the beginning have no growth except what depended on the will of its master.

The founders of cities are independent when they are people who, under the leadership of some prince, or by themselves, have been obliged to fly from pestilence, war, or famine, that was desolating their native country, and are seeking a new home. These either inhabit the cities of the country of which they take possession, as Moses did; or they build new ones, as was done by Æneas. In such case we are able to appreciate the talents of the founder and the success of his work, which is more or less remarkable according as he, in founding the city, displays more or less wisdom and skill. Both the one and the other are recognized by the selection of the place where he has located the city, and by the nature of the laws which he establishes in it. And as men work either from necessity or from choice, and as it has been observed that virtue has more sway where labor is the result of necessity rather than of choice, it is a matter of consideration whether it might not be better to select for the establishment of a city a sterile region, where the people, compelled by necessity to be industrious, and therefore less given to idleness, would be more united, and less exposed by the poverty of the country to occasions for discord; as was the case with Ragusa, and several other cities that were built upon an ungrateful soil. Such a selection of site would doubtless be more useful and wise if men were content with what they possess, and did not desire to exercise command over others.

Now, as people cannot make themselves secure except by being powerful, it is necessary in the founding of a city to avoid a sterile country. . . . As to the idleness which the fertility of a country tends to encourage, the laws should compel men to labor where the sterility of the soil does not do it; as was done by those skilful and sagacious legislators who have inhabited very agreeable and fertile countries, such as are apt to make men idle and unfit for the exercise of valor. . . .

I say, then, that for the establishment of a city it is wisest to select the most fertile spot, especially as the laws can prevent the ill effects that would otherwise result from that very fertility. . . .

Chapter II

OF THE DIFFERENT KINDS OF REPUBLICS, AND
OF WHAT KIND THE ROMAN REPUBLIC WAS

I will leave aside what might be said of cities which from their very birth have been subject to a foreign power, and will speak only of those whose origin has been independent, and which from the first governed themselves by their own laws, whether as republics or as principalities, and whose constitution and laws have differed as their origin. Some have had at the very beginning, or soon after, a legislator, who, like Lycurgus with the Lacedæmonians, gave them by a single act all the laws they needed. Others have owed theirs to chance and to events, and have received their laws at different times, as Rome did. It is a great good fortune for a republic to have a legislator sufficiently wise to give her laws so regulated that, without the necessity of correcting them, they afford security to those who live under them. Sparta observed her laws for more than eight hundred years without altering them and without experiencing a single dangerous disturbance. Unhappy, on the contrary, is that republic which, not having at the beginning fallen into the hands of a sagacious and skilful legislator, is herself obliged to reform her laws. More unhappy still is that republic which from the first has diverged from a good constitution. And that republic is furthest from it whose vicious institutions impede her progress, and make her leave the right path that leads to a good end; for those who are in that condition can hardly ever be brought into the right road. Those republics, on the other hand, that started without having even a perfect constitution, but made a fair beginning, and are capable of improvement,—such republics, I say, may perfect themselves by the aid of events. It is very true, however, that such reforms are never effected without danger, for the majority of men never willingly adopt any new law tending to change the constitution of the state, unless the necessity of the change is clearly demonstrated; and as such a necessity cannot make itself felt without being accompanied with danger, the republic may easily be destroyed before having perfected its constitution. That of Florence is a complete proof of this: reorganized after the revolt of Arezzo, in 1502, it was overthrown after the taking of Prato, in 1512.

Having proposed to myself to treat of the kind of government established at Rome, and of the events that led to its perfection, I must at the beginning observe that some of the writers on politics distinguished three kinds of government, viz. the monarchical, the aristocratic, and the democratic; and maintain that the legislators of a people must choose from these three the one that seems to them most suitable. Other authors, wiser according to the opinion of many, count six kinds of governments, three of which are very bad, and three good in themselves, but so liable to be corrupted that they become absolutely bad. The three good ones are those which we have just named; the three bad ones result from the degradation of the other three, and each of them resembles its corresponding original, so that the transition from the one to the other is very easy.

Thus monarchy becomes tyranny; aristocracy degenerates into oligarchy; and the popular government lapses readily into licentiousness. So that a legislator who gives to a state which he founds, either of these three forms of government, constitutes it but for a brief time; for no precautions can prevent either one of the three that are reputed good, from degenerating into its opposite kind; so great are in these the attractions and resemblances between the good and the evil. . . .

. . . I say, then, that all kinds of government are defective; those three which we have qualified as good because they are too short-lived, and the three bad ones because of their inherent viciousness. Thus sagacious legislators, knowing the vices of each of these systems of government by themselves, have chosen one that should partake of all of them, judging that to be the most stable and solid. In fact, when there is combined under the same constitution a prince, a nobility, and the power of the people, then these three powers will watch and keep each other reciprocally in check.

Amongst those justly celebrated for having established such a constitution, Lycurgus beyond doubt merits the highest praise. He organized the government of Sparta in such manner that, in giving to the king, the nobles, and the people each their portion of authority and duties, he created a government which maintained itself for over eight hundred years in the most perfect tranquility, and reflected infinite glory upon this legislator. On the other hand, the constitution given by Solon to the Athenians, by which he established only a popular government, was of such short duration that before his death he saw the tyranny of Pisistratus arise. And although forty years afterwards the heirs of the tyrant were expelled, so that Athens recovered her liberties and restored the popular government according to the laws of Solon, yet it did not last over a hundred years; although a number of laws that had been overlooked by Solon were adopted, to maintain the government against the insolence of the nobles and the license of the populace. The fault he had committed in not tempering the power of the people and that of the prince and his nobles, made the duration of the government of Athens very short, as compared with that of Sparta.

But let us come to Rome. Although she had no legislator like Lycurgus, who constituted her government, at her very origin, in a manner to secure her liberty for a length of time, yet the disunion which existed between the Senate and the people produced such extraordinary events, that chance did for her what the laws had failed to do. Thus, if Rome did not attain the first degree of happiness, she at least had the second. Her first institutions were doubtless defective, but they were not in conflict with the principles that might bring her to perfection.

. . . Fortune favored her, so that, although the authority passed successively from the kings and nobles to the people, by the same degrees and for the same reasons that we have spoken of, yet the royal authority was never entirely abolished to bestow it upon the nobles; and these were never entirely deprived of their authority to give it to the people; but a combination was formed of the three powers, which rendered the constitution perfect, and this perfection was attained by the disunion of the Senate and the people, as we shall more fully show in the following two chapters.

Chapter III

OF THE EVENTS THAT CAUSED THE CREATION

OF TRIBUNES IN ROME; WHICH MADE

THE REPUBLIC MORE PERFECT

All those who have written upon civil institutions demonstrate (and history is full of examples to support them) that whoever desires to found a state and give it laws, must start with assuming that all men are bad and ever ready to display their vicious nature, whenever they may find occasion for it. If their evil disposition remains concealed for a time, it must be attributed to some unknown reason; and we must assume that it lacked occasion to show itself; but time, which has been said to be the father of all truth, does not fail to bring it to light. . . .

Chapter IV

THE DISUNION OF THE SENATE AND THE PEOPLE

RENDERS THE REPUBLIC OF ROME POWERFUL AND FREE

I shall not pass over in silence the disturbances that occurred in Rome from the time of the death of the Tarquins to that of the creation of the Tribunes; and shall afterwards refute the opinion of those who claim that the Roman republic has always been a theatre of turbulence and disorder, and that if its extreme good fortune and the military discipline had not supplied the defects of her constitution, she would have deserved the lowest rank amongst the republics.

It cannot be denied that the Roman Empire was the result of good fortune and military discipline; but it seems to me that it ought to be perceived that where good discipline prevails there also will good order prevail, and good fortune rarely fails to follow in their train. Let us, however, go into details upon this point. I maintain that those who blame the quarrels of the Senate and the people of Rome condemn that which was the very origin of liberty, and that they were probably more impressed by the cries and noise which these disturbances occasioned in the public places, than by the good effect which they produced; and that they do not consider that in every republic there are two parties, that of the nobles and that of the people; and all the laws that are favorable to liberty result from the opposition of these parties to each other, as may easily be seen from the events that occurred in Rome. From the time of the Tarquins to that of the Gracchi, that is to say, within the space of over three hundred years, the differences between these parties caused but very few exiles, and cost still less blood; they cannot therefore be regarded as having been very injurious and fatal to a republic, which during the course of so many years saw on this account only eight or ten of its citizens sent into exile, and but a very small number put to death, and even but a few condemned to pecuniary fines. Nor can we regard a republic as disorderly where so many virtues were seen to shine. For good examples are the result of good education, and good education is due to good laws; and good laws in their turn spring from those very agitations which have been so inconsiderately condemned by many. For whoever will carefully examine the result of these agitations will find that they have neither caused exiles nor any violence prejudicial to the general good, and will be convinced even that they have given rise to laws that were to the advantage of public liberty. And if it be said that these are strange means,— to hear constantly the cries of the people furious against the Senate, and of a Senate declaiming against the people, to see the populace rush tumultuously through the streets, close their houses, and even leave the city of

Rome,—I reply, that all these things can alarm only those who read of them, and that every free state ought to afford the people the opportunity of giving vent, so to say, to their ambition; and above all those republics which on important occasions have to avail themselves of this very people. Now such were the means employed at Rome; when the people wanted to obtain a law, they resorted to some of the extremes of which we have just spoken, or they refused to enroll themselves to serve in the wars, so that the Senate was obliged to satisfy them in some measure. The demands of a free people are rarely pernicious to their liberty; they are generally inspired by oppressions, experienced or apprehended; and if their fears are ill founded, resort is had to public assemblies where the mere eloquence of a single good and respectable man will make them sensible of their error. "The people," says Cicero, "although ignorant, yet are capable of appreciating the truth, and yield to it readily when it is presented to them by a man whom they esteem worthy of their confidence."

One should show then more reserve in blaming the Roman government, and consider that so many good effects, which originated in that republic, cannot but result from very good causes. If the troubles of Rome occasioned the creation of Tribunes, then they cannot be praised too highly; for besides giving to the people a share in the public administration, these Tribunes were established as the most assured guardians of Roman liberty, as we shall see in the following chapter.

Chapter V

TO WHOM CAN THE GUARDIANSHIP OF LIBERTY MORE
SAFELY BE CONFIDED, TO THE NOBLES OR TO THE
PEOPLE? AND WHICH OF THE TWO HAVE MOST CAUSE
FOR CREATING DISTURBANCES THOSE WHO WISH TO
ACQUIRE, OR THOSE WHO DESIRE TO CONSERVE?

All the legislators that have given wise constitutions to republics have deemed it an essential precaution to establish a guard and protection to liberty; and according as this was more or less wisely placed, liberty endured a greater or less length of time. As every republic was composed of nobles and people, the question arose as to whose hands it was best to confide the protection of liberty. The Lacedæmonians, and in our day the Venetians, gave it into the hands of the nobility; but the Romans intrusted it to the people. We must examine, therefore, which of these republics made the best choice. There are strong reasons in favor of each, but, to judge by the results, we must incline in favor of the nobles, for the liberties of Sparta and Venice endured a longer space of time than those of Rome. But to come to the reasons, taking the part of Rome first, I will say, that one should always confide any deposit to those who have least desire of violating it; and doubtless, if we consider the objects of the nobles and of the people, we must see that the first have a great desire to dominate, whilst the latter have only the wish not to be dominated, and consequently a greater desire to live in the enjoyment of liberty; so that when the people are intrusted with the care of any privilege or liberty, being less disposed to encroach upon it, they will of necessity take better care of it; and being unable to take it away themselves, will prevent others from doing so.

On the contrary, it is said, in favor of the course adopted by Sparta and Venice, that the preference given to the nobility, as guardians of public liberty, has two advantages: the first, to yield something to the ambition of those who, being more engaged in the management of public affairs, find, so to say, in the weapon which the office places in their hands, a means of power that satisfies them; the other, to deprive the restless spirit of the masses of an authority calculated from its very nature to produce trouble and dissensions, and apt to drive the nobles to some act of desperation, which in time may cause the greatest misfortunes. Rome is even adduced as an example of this; for having confided, it is said, this authority to the tribunes of the people, these were seen not to be content with having only one Consul taken from this class, but wanted both to be plebeians. They afterwards claimed the Censure, the Prætoriate, and all the other dignities of the republic. And not satisfied with these advantages, and urged on by the same violence, they came in the end to idolize all those whom they saw disposed to attack the nobles, which gave rise to the power of Marius and to the ruin of Rome.

And, truly, whoever weighs all these reasons accurately may well remain in doubt which of the two classes he would choose as the guardians of liberty, not knowing which would be least dangerous,—those who seek to acquire an authority which they have not, or those who desire to preserve that which they already possess. After the nicest examination, this is what I think may be concluded from it. The question refers either to a republic that desires to extend its empire, as Rome, or to a state that confines itself merely to its own preservation. In the first case Rome should be imitated, and in the second the example of Sparta and Venice should be followed; and in the next chapter we shall see the reasons why and the means by which this is to be done.

To come back now to the question as to which men are most dangerous in a republic, those who wish to acquire power or those who fear to lose that which they possess, I will remark that Menenius and M. Fulvius, both plebeians, were named, the one Dictator and the other Commander of the Cavalry, to make investigations on the occasion of a conspiracy formed at Capua against Rome. They were also commissioned to find out all those who from ambition and by extraordinary means sought to obtain the Consulate and the other important offices of the republic. The nobility, believing that such an authority given to the Dictator was aimed against them, spread the report throughout the city that it was not they who sought thus to arrive at these honors from ambition or by illicit proceedings, but rather the plebeians, who, trusting neither to their birth nor their personal merits, thus employed extraordinary means to obtain these honors, and they particularly charged it upon the Dictator himself. This accusation was so actively followed up that Menenius felt himself obliged to convoke an assembly of the people; where, after having complained of the calumnies spread against him by the nobles, he deposed the Dictatorship and submitted himself to the judgment of the people. The cause having been pleaded, Menenius was absolved. On that occasion there was much discussion as to which was the most ambitious, he who wished to preserve power or he who wished to acquire it; as both the one and the other of these motives may be the cause of great troubles. It seems, however, that they are most frequently occasioned by those who possess; for the fear to lose stirs the same passions in men as the desire to gain, as men do not believe themselves sure of what they already possess except by acquiring still more; and, moreover, these new acquisitions are so many means of strength and power for abuses; and what is still worse is that the haughty manners and insolence of the nobles and the rich excite in the breasts of those who have neither birth nor wealth, not only the desire to possess them, but also the wish to revenge themselves by depriving the former of those riches and honors which they see them employ so badly.

Chapter IX

TO FOUND A NEW REPUBLIC, OR TO REFORM ENTIRELY
THE OLD INSTITUTIONS OF AN EXISTING ONE,
MUST BE THE WORK OF ONE MAN ONLY

It may perhaps appear to some that I have gone too far into the details of Roman history before having made any mention of the founders of that republic, or of her institutions, her religion, and her military establishment. Not wishing, therefore, to keep any longer in suspense the desires of those who wish to understand these matters, I say that many will perhaps consider it an evil example that the founder of a civil society, as Romulus was, should first have killed his brother, and then have consented to the death of Titus Tatius, who had been elected to share the royal authority with him; from which it might be concluded that the citizens, according to the example of their prince, might, from ambition and the desire to rule, destroy those who attempt to oppose their authority. This opinion would be correct, if we do not take into consideration the object which

Romulus had in view in committing that homicide. But we must assume, as a general rule, that it never or rarely happens that a republic or monarchy is well constituted, or its old institutions entirely reformed, unless it is done by only one individual; it is even necessary that he whose mind has conceived such a constitution should be alone in carrying it into effect. A sagacious legislator of a republic, therefore, whose object is to promote the public good, and not his private interests, and who prefers his country to his own successors, should concentrate all authority in himself; and a wise mind will never censure any one for having employed any extraordinary means for the purpose of establishing a kingdom or constituting a republic. It is well that, when the act accuses him, the result should excuse him; and when the result is good, as in the case of Romulus, it will always absolve him from blame. For he is to be reprehended who commits violence for the purpose of destroying, and not he who employs it for beneficent purposes. The lawgiver should, however, be sufficiently wise and virtuous not to leave this authority which he has assumed either to his heirs or to any one else; for mankind, being more prone to evil than to good, his successor might employ for evil purposes the power which he had used only for good ends. Besides, although one man alone should organize a government, yet it will not endure long if the administration of it remains on the shoulders of a single individual; it is well, then, to confide this to the charge of many, for thus it will be sustained by the many. . . .

The above views might be corroborated by any number of examples, such as those of Moses, Lycurgus, Solon, and other founders of monarchies and republics, who were enabled to establish laws suitable for the general good only by keeping for themselves an exclusive authority; but all these are so well known that I will not further refer to them. . . .

Chapter X

IN PROPORTION AS THE FOUNDERS OF A REPUBLIC OR MONARCHY ARE ENTITLED TO PRAISE, SO DO THE FOUNDERS OF A TYRANNY DESERVE EXECRATION

Of all men who have been eulogized, those deserve it most who have been the authors and founders of religions; next come such as have established republics or kingdoms. After these the most celebrated are those who have commanded armies, and have extended the possessions of their kingdom or country. To these may be added literary men, but, as these are of different kinds, they are celebrated according to their respective degrees of excellence. All others—and their number is infinite—receive such share of praise as pertains to the exercise of their arts and professions. On the contrary, those are doomed to infamy and universal execration who have destroyed religions, who have overturned republics and kingdoms, who are enemies of virtue, of letters, and of every art that is useful and honorable to mankind. Such are the impious and violent, the ignorant, the idle, the vile and degraded. And there are none so foolish or so wise, so wicked or so good, that, in choosing between these two qualities, they do not praise what is praiseworthy and blame that which deserves blame. And yet nearly all men, deceived by a false good and a false glory, allow themselves voluntarily or ignorantly to be drawn towards those who deserve more blame than praise. . . .

Chapter XI

OF THE RELIGION OF THE ROMANS

Although the founder of Rome was Romulus, to whom like a daughter, she owed her birth and her education, yet the gods did not judge the laws of this prince sufficient for so great an empire, and therefore inspired the Roman Senate to elect Numa Pompilius as his successor, so that he might regulate all those things that had been omitted by Romulus. Numa, finding a very savage people, and wishing to reduce them to civil obedience by the arts of peace, had recourse to religion as the most necessary and assured support of any civil society; and he established it upon such foundations that for many centuries there was nowhere more fear of the gods than in that republic, which greatly facilitated all the enterprises which the Senate or its great men attempted. Whoever will examine the actions of the people of Rome as a body, or of many individual Romans will see that these citizens feared much more to break an oath than the laws; like men who esteem the power of the gods more than that of men. . . . In truth, there never was any remarkable lawgiver amongst any people who did not resort to divine authority, as otherwise his laws would not have been accepted by the people; for there are many good laws, the importance of which is known to the sagacious lawgiver, but the reasons for which are not sufficiently evident to enable him to persuade others to submit to them; and therefore do wise men, for the purpose of removing this difficulty, resort to divine authority. Thus did Lycurgus and Solon, and many others who aimed at the same thing. . . .

Chapter XII

THE IMPORTANCE OF GIVING RELIGION A PROMINENT
INFLUENCE IN A STATE, AND HOW ITALY WAS RUINED
BECAUSE SHE FAILED IN THIS RESPECT THROUGH THE
CONDUCT OF THE CHURCH OF ROME

Princes and republics who wish to maintain themselves free from corruption must above all things preserve the purity of all religious observances, and treat them with proper reverence; for there is no greater indication of the ruin of a country than to see religion contemned. And this is easily understood, when we know upon what the religion of a country is founded; for the essence of every religion is based upon some one main principle. . . .

And certainly, if the Christian religion had from the beginning been maintained according to the principles of its founder, the Christian states and republics would have been much more united and happy than what they are. Nor can there be a greater proof of its decadence than to witness the fact that the nearer people are to the Church of Rome, which is the head of our religion, the less religious are they. And whoever examines the principles upon which that religion is founded, and sees how widely different from those principles its present practice and application are, will judge that her ruin or chastisement is near at hand. But as there are some of the opinion that the well-being of Italian affairs depends upon the Church of Rome, I will present such arguments against that opinion as occur to me; two of which are most important, and cannot according to my judgment be controverted. The first is, that the evil example of the court of Rome has destroyed all piety and religion in Italy, which brings in its train infinite improprieties and disorders; for as we may presuppose all good where religion prevails, so where it is wanting we have the right to suppose the very opposite. We Italians then owe to the Church of Rome and to her priests our having become irreligious and bad; but we owe her a still greater debt, and one that will be the cause of our ruin, namely, that the Church has kept and still keeps our country divided. And certainly a country can never be united and happy, except when it obeys wholly one government, whether a republic or a monarchy, as is the case in France and in Spain; and the sole cause why Italy is not in the same condition, and is not governed by either one republic or one sovereign, is the Church; for having acquired and holding a temporal dominion, yet she has never had sufficient power or courage to enable her to seize the rest of the country and make herself sole sovereign of all Italy. And on the other hand she has not been so feeble that the fear of losing her temporal power prevented her from calling in the aid of a foreign power to defend her against such others as had become too powerful in Italy; as was seen in former days by many sad experiences, when through the intervention of Charlemagne she drove out the Lombards, who were masters of nearly all Italy; and when in our times she crushed the power of the Venetians by the aid of France, and afterwards with the assistance of the Swiss drove out in turn the French. The Church, then, not having been powerful enough to be able to master all Italy, nor having permitted any other power to do so, has been the cause why Italy has never been able to unite under one head, but has always remained under a number of princes and lords, which occasioned her so many dissensions and so much weakness that she became a prey not only to the powerful barbarians, but of whoever chose to assail her. This we other Italians owe to the Church of Rome, and to none other. And any one, to be promptly convinced by experiment of the truth of all this, should have the power to transport the court of Rome to reside, with all the power it has in Italy, in the midst of the Swiss, who of all peoples nowadays live most according to their ancient customs so far as religion and their military system are concerned; and he would see in a very little while that the evil habits of that court would create more confusion in that country than anything else that could ever happen there.

Chapter XIV

THE ROMANS INTERPRETED THE AUSPICES ACCORDING TO NECESSITY, AND VERY WISELY MADE SHOW OF OBSERVING RELIGION, EVEN WHEN THEY WERE OBLIGED IN REALITY TO DISREGARD IT; AND IF ANY ONE RECKLESSLY DISPARAGED IT, HE WAS PUNISHED

The system of auguries was not only, as we have said above, the principal basis of the ancient religion of the Gentiles, but was also the cause of the prosperity of the Roman republic. Whence the Romans esteemed it more than any other institution, and resorted to it in their Consular Comitii, in commencing any important enterprise, in sending armies into the field, in ordering their battles, and in every other important civil or military action. Nor would they ever have ventured upon any expedition unless the augurs had first persuaded the soldiers that the gods promised them victory. Amongst other auspices the armies were always accompanied by a certain class of soothsayers, termed Pollari (guardians of the sacred fowls), and every time before giving battle to the enemy, they required these Pollari to ascertain the auspices; and if the fowls ate freely, then it was deemed a favorable augury, and the soldiers fought confidently, but if the fowls refuses to eat, then they abstained from battle. Nevertheless, when they saw a good reason why certain things should be done, they did them anyhow, whether the auspices were favorable or not; but then they turned and interpreted the auguries so artfully, and in such manner, that seemingly no disrespect was shown to their religious belief. . . .

Chapter XVII

A CORRUPT PEOPLE THAT BECOMES FREE CAN WITH GREATEST DIFFICULTY MAINTAIN ITS LIBERTY

I think that it was necessary for royalty to be extinguished in Rome, else she would in a very short time have become feeble and devoid of energy. For the degree of corruption to which the kings had sunk was such that, if it had continued for two or three successive reigns, and had extended from the head to the members of the body so that these had become also corrupt, it would have been impossible ever to have reformed the state. But losing the head whilst the trunk was still sound, it was easy to restore Rome to liberty and proper institutions. And it must be assumed as a well-demonstrated truth, that a corrupt people that lives under the government of a prince can never become free, even though the prince and his whole line should be extinguished; and that it would be better that the one prince should be destroyed by another. For a people in such condition can never become settled unless a new prince be created, who by his good qualities and valor can maintain their liberty; but even then it will last only during the lifetime of the new prince. It was thus that the freedom of Syracuse was preserved at different times by the valor of Dion and Timoleon during their lives, but after their death the city relapsed under the former tyranny. But there is not a more striking example of this than Rome itself, which after the expulsion of the Tarquins was enabled quickly to resume and maintain her liberty; but after the death of Cæsar, Caligula, and Nero, and after the extinction of the entire Cæsarean line, she could not even begin to re-establish her liberty, and much less preserve it. And this great difference in the condition of things in one and the same city resulted entirely from this fact, that at the time of the Tarquins the Roman people was not yet corrupt, whilst under the Cæsars it became corrupt to the lowest degree. . . .

Chapter XXVII

SHOWING THAT MEN ARE VERY RARELY EITHER
ENTIRELY GOOD OR ENTIRELY BAD

When Pope Julius II went, in the year 1505, to Bologna to expel the Bentivogli from that state, the government of which they had held for a hundred years, he wanted also to remove Giovanpaolo Baglioni from Perugia, who had made himself the absolute master of that city; for it was the intention of Pope Julius to destroy all the petty tyrants that occupied the possessions of the Church. Having arrived at Perugia with that purpose, which was well known to everybody, he did not wait to enter the city with his army for his protection, but went in almost alone, although Giovanpaolo had collected a large force within the city for his defence. And thus, with the customary impetuosity which characterized all his acts, Julius placed himself with only a small guard in the hands of his enemy Baglioni, whom he nevertheless carried off with him, leaving a governor in his stead to administer the state in the name of the Church. Sagacious men who were with the Pope observed his temerity and the cowardice of Baglioni, and could not understand why the latter had not by a single blow rid himself of his enemy, whereby he would have secured for himself eternal fame and rich booty, for the Pope was accompanied by all the cardinals with their valuables. Nor could they believe that he had refrained from doing this either from goodness or conscientious scruples; for no sentiment of piety or respect could enter the heart of a man of such vile character as Giovanpaolo, who had dishonored his sister and murdered his nephews and cousins for the sake of obtaining possession of the state; but they concluded that mankind were neither utterly wicked nor perfectly good, and that when a crime has in itself some grandeur or magnanimity they will not know how to attempt it. Thus Giovanpaolo Baglioni, who did not mind open incest and parricide, knew not how, or, more correctly speaking, dared not, to attempt an act (although having a justifiable opportunity) for which every one would have admired his courage, and which would have secured him eternal fame, as being the first to show these prelates how little esteem those merit who live and govern as they do; and as having done an act the greatness of which would have overshadowed the infamy and all the danger that could possibly result from it.

Chapter XXIX

WHICH OF THE TWO IS MOST UNGRATEFUL,

A PEOPLE OR A PRINCE

It seems to me proper here, in connection with the above subject, to examine whether the people or a prince is more liable to the charge of ingratitude; and by way of illustrating this question the better, I set out by saying that the vice of ingratitude springs either from avarice or fear. For when a people or a prince has sent a general on some important expedition where by his success he acquires great glory, the prince or people is in turn bound to reward him. But if instead of such reward they dishonor and wrong him, influenced thereto by avarice, then they are guilty of an inexcusable wrong, which will involve them in eternal infamy. And yet there are many princes who commit this wrong, for which fact Tacitus assigns the reason in the following sentence: "Men are more ready to repay an injury than a benefit, because gratitude is a burden and revenge a pleasure." But when they fail to reward, or rather when they offend, not from avarice, but from suspicion and fear, then the people or the prince have some excuse for their ingratitude. We read of many instances of this kind; for the general who by his valor has conquered a state for his master, and won great glory for himself by his victory over the enemy, and has loaded his soldiers with rich booty, acquires necessarily with his own soldiers, as well as with those of the enemy and with the subjects of the prince, so high a reputation, that his very victory may become distasteful, and a cause for apprehension to his prince. For as the nature of men is ambitious as well as suspicious, and puts no limits to one's good fortune, it is not impossible that the suspicion that may suddenly be aroused in the mind of the prince by the victory of the general may have been aggravated by some haughty expressions or insolent acts on his part; so that the prince will naturally be made to think of securing himself against the ambition of his general. And to do this, the means that suggest themselves to him are either to have the general killed, or to deprive him of that reputation which he has acquired with the prince's army and the people, by using every means to prove that the general's victory was not due to his skill and courage, but to chance and the cowardice of the enemy, or to the sagacity of the other captains who were with him in that action. . . .

Fear and suspicion are so natural to princes that they cannot defend themselves against them, and thus it is impossible for them to show gratitude to those who, by victories achieved under their banners, have made important conquests for them. If then a prince cannot prevent himself from committing such wrongs, it is surely no wonder, nor matter worthy of more consideration, if a people acts in a similar manner. . . .

. . . I say that, as the vice of ingratitude is usually the consequence of either avarice or fear, it will be seen that the peoples never fall into this error for avarice, and that fear also makes them less liable to it than princes, inasmuch as they have less reason for fear, as we shall show further on.

SECOND BOOK

Chapter I

THE GREATNESS OF THE ROMANS WAS DUE MORE TO
THEIR VALOR AND ABILITY THAN TO GOOD FORTUNE

Many authors, amongst them that most serious writer
Plutarch, have held the opinion that the people of Rome
were more indebted in the acquisition of their empire to
the favors of Fortune than to their own merits. And
amongst other reasons adduced by Plutarch is, that by
their own confession it appears that the Roman people
ascribed all their victories to Fortune, because they
built more temples to that goddess than to any other
deity. It seems that Livius accepts that opinion, for he
rarely makes a Roman speak of valor without coupling
fortune with it. Now I do not share that opinion at all,
and do not believe that it can be sustained; for if no
other republic has ever been known to make such conquests, it is admitted that none other was so well organized for that purpose as Rome. It was the valor of her
armies that achieved those conquests, but it was the wisdom of her conduct and the nature of her institutions,
as established by her first legislator, that enabled her to
preserve these acquisitions, as we shall more fully set
forth in the succeeding chapters. But it is said that the
fact that the Roman people never had two important
wars on hand at the same time was due more to their

good fortune than their wisdom; for they did not engage in war with the Latins until they had beaten the Samnites so completely that the Romans themselves had to protect them with their arms; nor did they combat the Tuscans until after they had subjugated the Latins, and had by repeated defeats completely enervated the Samnites. Doubtless if these two powerful nations had united against Rome whilst their strength was yet unbroken, it may readily be supposed that they could have destroyed the Roman republic. . . .

Chapter XVII

OF THE VALUE OF ARTILLERY TO MODERN ARMIES,
AND WHETHER THE GENERAL OPINION
RESPECTING IT IS CORRECT

Considering the many open field fights, or pitched battles as they are called in our day, that were fought by the Romans at various times, I have reflected upon the opinion so universally entertained, that, if artillery had existed in ancient times, the Romans would not have been allowed so easily to conquer provinces and make other peoples tributary to themselves; nor would they in any way have been able to extend their dominions so largely. It is further said, that the use of these fire-arms prevents men from displaying the same personal valor as they could in ancient times; that it is more difficult to join battle than formerly, and that the same organization and discipline of armies cannot be preserved; and that henceforth the battles will be fought mainly by artillery. I deem it, therefore, not from our purpose to examine whether these opinions are correct, and in how far the introduction of artillery has increased or diminished the strength of armies, and whether it gives or takes away from good commanders the opportunity of acting valiantly. . . .

. . . I will conclude this chapter, therefore, by saying that artillery is useful in an army when the soldiers are animated by the same valor as that of the ancient Romans, but without that it is perfectly inefficient, especially against courageous troops.

Chapter XXIV

FORTRESSES ARE GENERALLY MORE
INJURIOUS THAN USEFUL

It may perhaps seem to the learned men of our time that the Romans acted without proper consideration when, in their desire to make sure of the people of Latium and of the city of Privernum, they did not build some fortresses there to serve as a check, and as a guaranty of their fidelity; especially as it is a general saying of our wiseacres in Florence that Pisa and other similar cities should be held by citadels. Doubtless, if the Romans had been of the same composition, they would have constructed fortresses; but as they were men of very dif-

ferent courage, judgment, and power, they did not build
them. And so long as Rome was free, and adhered to
her old customs and admirable constitution, they never
built fortresses to hold either cities or countries which
they had conquered, although they preserved some of
the strong places which they found already existing.
Seeing, then, the mode of proceeding of the Romans in
this respect, and that of the princes of our present time,
it seems to me proper to examine whether it is well to
build fortresses, and whether they are of benefit or
injury to him who builds them. We must consider, then,
the object of fortresses, with reference to their serving
as a means of defence against a foreign enemy as well as
against one's own subjects.

In the first case, I maintain they are unnecessary,
and in the second decidedly injurious. . . .

. . . A prince then, who can raise a good army, need
not build any fortresses; and one who cannot should
not build any. It is proper enough that he should fortify
the city in which he resides, so as to be able to resist the
first shock of an enemy, and to afford himself the time
to negotiate, or to obtain aid from without for his
relief; but anything more is mere waste of money in
time of peace, and useless in time of war. And thus
whoever reflects upon all I have said upon the subject
will see that the same wisdom which inspired the
Romans in all other matters equally guided them in

their decisions respecting the Latins and the Privernati, when, instead of relying upon fortresses, they secured the allegiance of these people by wiser and more magnanimous means.

THIRD BOOK

Chapter I

TO INSURE A LONG EXISTENCE TO RELIGIOUS SECTS OR REPUBLICS, IT IS NECESSARY FREQUENTLY TO BRING THEM BACK TO THEIR ORIGINAL PRINCIPLES

There is nothing more true than that all the things of this world have a limit to their existence; but those only run the entire course ordained for them by Heaven that do not allow their body to become disorganized, but keep it unchanged in the manner ordained, or if they change it, so do it that it shall be for their advantage, and not to their injury. And as I speak here of mixed bodies, such as republics or religious sects, I say that those changes are beneficial that bring them back to their original principles. And those are the best-constituted bodies, and have the longest existence, which possess the intrinsic means of frequently renewing themselves, or such as obtain this renovation in consequence of some extrinsic accidents. And it is a truth clearer than light that, without such renovation, these bodies cannot continue to exist; and the means of renewing them is to bring them back to their original principles. For, as all religious republics and monarchies must have within themselves some goodness, by means of which they obtain their first growth and reputation, and as in the process of time this goodness becomes corrupted, it will of necessity destroy the body unless something intervenes to bring it back to its normal condition. Thus, the doctors of medicine say, in speaking of the human body, that "every day some ill humors gather which must be cured."

This return of a republic to its original principles is either the result of extrinsic accident or of intrinsic prudence. As an instance of the first, we have seen how necessary it was that Rome should be taken by the Gauls, as a means of her renovation or new birth; so that, being thus born again, she might take new life and vigor, and might resume the proper observance of justice and religion, which were becoming corrupt. . . .

We may conclude, then, that nothing is more necessary for an association of men, either as a religious sect, republic, or monarchy, than to restore to it from time to time the power and reputation which it had in the beginning, and to strive to have either good laws or good men to bring about such a result, without the necessity of the intervention of any extrinsic force. For although such may at times be the best remedy, as in the case of Rome (when captured by the Gauls), yet it is so dangerous that it is in no way desirable. . . .

Chapter XLVII

LOVE OF COUNTRY SHOULD MAKE A GOOD
CITIZEN FORGET PRIVATE WRONGS

The Consul Manlius was wounded in a fight during the war against the Samnites, and as his army, in consequence of his being disabled, were exposed to great danger, the Roman Senate judged it necessary to send Papirius Cursor as Dictator to supply the place of the Consul. But as the law required that the Dictator should be named by Fabius, who was at that time at the head of the armies in Tuscany, and being known to be hostile to Papirius, the Senate feared that he might refuse to nominate him. They therefore sent two deputies to entreat him to put aside his personal hatreds, and to nominate Papirius Consul for the general good. Moved by his love of country, Fabius made that nomination, although he manifested, by his silence and other indications, his aversion to him. This should serve as an example to all who desire to be regarded as good citizens.

Chapter XLIX

A REPUBLIC THAT DESIRES TO MAINTAIN HER
LIBERTIES NEEDS DAILY FRESH PRECAUTIONS:
IT WAS BY SUCH MERITS THAT FABIUS OBTAINED
THE SURNAME OF MAXIMUS

We have already said elsewhere, that in a great republic there are constantly evils occurring requiring remedies which must be efficacious in proportion to the importance of the occasion. And if ever any city experienced strange and unforeseen ills, it was Rome. Such, for instance, as the plot which the Roman ladies seem to have formed to kill their husbands, so that many had actually poisoned them, whilst others had prepared the poison for the purpose. Such was also the conspiracy of the Bacchanals, discovered at the time of the Macedonian war, in which many thousands of men and women were implicated. This conspiracy would have proved very dangerous to Rome had it not been discovered in time; and if the Romans had not been accustomed to punish the guilty, even if they were in great numbers. Even if we had not an infinity of other evidences of the greatness of this republic, it would be made manifest by the extent of her executions, and the character of the punishment she inflicted upon the guilty. Rome did not hesitate to have a whole legion put to death according to a judicial decision, or to destroy an entire city, or to send eight or ten thousand men into exile with such extraordinary conditions as could hardly be complied with by one man, much less by so many. . . . But the most terrible of her executions was the system of decimation in her armies, when, by lot, one soldier out of every ten was put to death. It was impossible to devise a more terrible punishment, where a great number were involved, than this. For when any crime is committed by a multitude, where the individual authors cannot be ascertained, it is impossible to punish them all, there being so many. To chastise a part, leaving the others unpunished, would be unjust to the first, whilst the others would feel encouraged to commit fresh crimes. But where all have merited death, and only every tenth man is punished by lot, these will have occasion to complain only of fate; whilst those who escape will be careful not to commit other crimes, for fear that the next time the lot might fall to them. The poisoners and the Bacchanals were punished as the greatness of their crimes merited.

About the Author

ALAN RYAN was born in London in 1940 and educated at Oxford University, where he taught for many
years. He was professor of politics at Princeton University from 1988 to 1996, and warden of New College,
Oxford University, and professor of political theory
from 1996 until 2009. He is the author of *The Philosophy
of John Stuart Mill*, *The Philosophy of the Social Sciences*, *J. S. Mill*,
Property and Political Theory, *Betrand Russell: A Political Life*,
John Dewey and the High Tide of American Liberalism, *Liberal
Anxieties and Liberal Education*, and *On Politics: A History of
Political Thought from Herodotus to the Present*. He is married
to Kate Ryan.